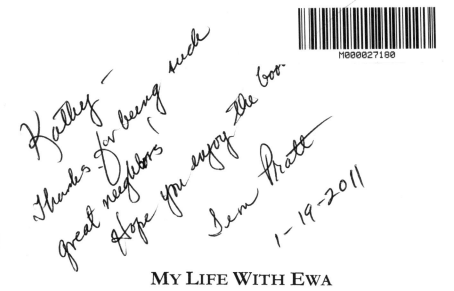

Kathy –
Thanks – for being such
great neighbors !
Hope you enjoy the boo-
Tim Pratt
1-19-2011

My Life With Ewa
The Early Years

Tim Pratt

Library Tales Publishing
www.librarytalespublishing,com

Copyright © 2009-2010 by Library Tales Publishing.
Library Tales Publishing, New York, NY, 10001

This Book's design is registered trademarks of Library Tales Publishing. Books may be purchased for business or sales promotional use. For information, please Email: Copyrights@Librarytales.com

ISBN: 978-0-578-05957-0

Printed in the United States of America

Acknowledgments

I would be totally remiss if I didn't recognize the many people who have helped me to see this project to fruition. Jerri Dahlman, Kelly Woods, and the administrative staff at McGladrey provided much-appreciated words of encouragement. Andrew Pratt served the multiple roles of instigator, editor, and critic. Usher Morgan's professional advice has been invaluable. My wife has endured my monopolization of our lone personal laptop computer. And my parents assisted with some of my recollections. Thank you to all.

Preface

What follows here is just as the title implies: an account of the early years of my life with my wife. The primary impetus for the project was provided by our son, Andrew. Having endured yet another retelling of our abridged response to the "How did you two meet?" question posed by some new acquaintances, he challenged me to write the story. Invariably, the answer to that specific question is summarized with a half dozen sentences, which encompass a four-year time period. With apologies to the late Paul Harvey, you are about to share in "the rest of the story." It has been a labor of love.

The inspiration for this effort has been the title character. She is one of a kind. I fear my words will fail to accurately describe that which makes her unique. Perhaps those who know her will share some of my observations.

I have released endorphins aplenty while revisiting old photo albums. I have learned much in the course of checking facts against my own recollections. I have watched less television. I have a sense of accomplishment at having completed what I started. Above all, I have, once again, affirmed that I am so very blessed to be married to my wife.

Tim Pratt

MY LIFE WITH EWA

For Andrew and Maya

Chapter 1: I'm Going Where?

It was May of 1975. Maybe you remember what it was like. The US was evacuating its embassy in Saigon. Streaking had come and gone. The stock market was just beginning to recover from an extended downturn. Gerald Ford was our president. Most people had yet to hear of Bruce Jenner. Jack Nicholson and *One Flew Over the Cuckoo's Nest* had just cleaned up at the Oscars. Nixon administration personnel were being sentenced to prison for their roles in Watergate. We were soon to reach two hundred years as a nation. The Cold War was going strong, but the "ping-pong diplomacy" of 1972 in China had initiated a thaw of sorts, even with the Soviet bloc. Eighteen was the legal age for drinking in many states. Simon and Garfunkel, Elton John, and the Eagles were among my personal favorites. The Pittsburgh Steelers had won their first Super Bowl in January. And I was driving a school bus twice a day to pay for tuition expenses at Grand View College before transferring to the University of Northern Iowa.

"You gotta be kidding me," I said to no one in particular as I pulled the bus on to the shoulder, in response to the flashing red lights that were clearly intended for me. I was usually the first driver to depart every afternoon from the Norwoodville Elementary School parking lot because my route covered the greatest distance. As the rookie driver I didn't select my route; it was assigned to me. I stood up to tell my kindergarten passengers to remain in their seats while I went back to the car with the flashing lights to talk with "Mr. Policeman."

Little Rollie Kouski asked, "Are you mad? My daddy always gets mad when he talks to the policeman."

I had to watch as every other driver slowed his bus to make certain he could believe what he was seeing. That's right, one of their very own was being cited for speeding—while driving a school bus full of kindergartners—less than three blocks from the school! Between their wild hand gestures and guffaws I was confident they would be waiting en masse at the bus barn once I finished the route. They were.

"Son, I've been sitting here in this same spot, every day, for two weeks. I've been watching all of you drivers barrel down Broadway. I know it is downhill, and I know the limit changes from twenty-five to forty-five just up the street. But right here it is only twenty-five. Every one of you drivers has been over the limit. I just decided that today I was going to send a message to all of you. You just happened to be the first one out of the chute, so I am citing you for speeding. Sorry, you were the one to be the example. Now maybe all of you will slow down."

And that is why I married a girl from Bydgoszcz, Poland.

I suppose that segue merits some explanation. My father always liked music. He was not a trained musician but he had a pleasant bass voice. He liked to sing and was in the church choir. But even when the choir wasn't singing, Dad always sang the hymns with a little more gusto than the rest of the congregation. And he would harmonize. That always fascinated me, too. You know how sometimes people sing really loud—like they are trying to impress you? Well, that wasn't Dad. If he had been like that I probably wouldn't have liked music. He just enjoyed singing, and still does. I wasn't particularly gifted in music, like my little sister was, but I was probably a little better than my older brother.

Dad found an outlet for his singing interests. He joined the Society for the Preservation and Encouragement of Barber Shop Quartet Singing in America Inc., or SPEBSQSA, for short. I was probably seven or eight years old when Mom and Dad took us to our first "Barbershop Show" at KRNT Theatre. I liked it. The music was OK, I guess, but I really liked those funny guys, "The Four Nubbins." (The featured quartet).

And that is why I married a girl from Bydgoszcz, Poland.

My youth was a pretty typical middle-America, 1960s, blue collar experience. We were probably closer to poor than to rich, but we were far from either one. Dad was a truck driver who had grown up with six siblings. Mom was a nurse and had been raised on a farm along with three sisters and a brother. We weren't exactly the Cleavers because Dad didn't wear a suit to work and Mom always worked outside the home to make ends meet. But Mom and Dad did teach some of the same values as Ward and June. My brother took care of me, kind of like Wally took care of The Beav. My father liked to reference my two best friends as Gilbert and Whitey. He even pegged another buddy as Eddie Haskell.

As I passed through adolescence, like most young men, I progressed from total insecurity to false confidence, to small bouts of genuine confidence. I had some great male role models. My dad and a couple of teachers and coaches let me know it was okay to pursue interests which may be out of the mainstream. I actually did a few things in school because I wondered if I would enjoy them, not because they were "the" things to do. I loved sports, but then, who didn't? I played football, baseball, and basketball, and I lifted weights. I'm not saying I was particularly good at any of those endeavors, but most guys did those things. No, I'm talking about learning to play chess… or bridge. I was the lead in a one act play that made it to state finals competition. I tried out for, and made, swing choir. I signed up for creative writing class. I was "Harry the Horse" in *Guys and Dolls*. I learned how to ballroom dance (I discovered girls love to dance and guys don't), and I became the youngest member of the DeMoinaires Barbershop Chorus.

I thought it was kind of cool to hang out with older guys every Monday night singing four-part a cappella harmony. To many it may sound weird to be seventeen or eighteen years old and be singing barbershop music with your dad and one of your uncles, but I enjoyed it. Besides, some of the guys would go for a beer after practice on Mondays. My dad didn't go. He didn't drink and the 6:00 AM start to his shift came too quickly. I had been doing this for a couple of years when the chorus was invited to be a part of some people-to-people diplomacy to Eastern Europe.

Like jazz, barbershop harmony is uniquely American. Some fellow named Owen Cash is credited with starting SPEBSQSA back in the 1930s. The story goes that the acronym was a spoof on the alphabet soup of acronyms resulting from FDR's New Deal programs of the Great Depression. SPEBSQSA changed its name a few years ago to the Barbershop Harmony Society and moved its national headquarters from Kenosha, Wisconsin, to Nashville, Tennessee. The DeMoinaires also changed their name to The Pride of Iowa Barbershop Chorus, but I digress.

Enculturation was a quasi government entity which had been established to promote people-to-people exchanges to countries which had generally been closed to Americans since the end of World War II. Someone had the great idea that if we were to send various slices of Americana to those faraway places, we could further melt the elements of the Cold War and make the world a safer place. So it was, when a representative of *Enculturation* came to the DeMoinaires to present an offer for our little barbershop chorus to travel to Poland for sixteen days in August/September of 1975.

The cost of the entire trip would be about seven hundred dollars per person, because much of it was being subsidized by the US and Polish governments, or at least that's how I remember things. The fact that Dad didn't have the vacation time only meant he didn't have to do the math to determine if he had the money. To me, seven hundred dollars may as well have been seven million. What little I knew of Poland generally began with, "How many Polacks does it take to…?" and that it was a communist country.

These challenges, combined with the fact that I was planning to be in Cedar Falls, Iowa, for the first week of my junior year of college before the chorus was scheduled to return, caused me to politely decline my

Uncle Vern's gracious offer to lend me the money for the trip. I had even made arrangements with the Cedar Falls Public Schools to drive a school bus while attending classes at the university, provided I came to school a week ahead of time for their bus driver orientation. The opportunity to take my first airplane ride was tempting, but I told Uncle Vern there was just no way.

So, there you have it. I was a middle class kid, living at home, finishing his sophomore year at the local junior college, enjoying barbershop as a hobby, and driving a school bus to earn money for the next year's tuition at the four year school. I had turned down the offer of a trip to some place behind the Iron Curtain because of insufficient funds and a requirement to be in Cedar Falls a week before classes were to start. Then some frustrated Polk County Deputy, who probably needed to make his quota, decided to interfere with my karma, touch me with that fickle finger of fate, and play havoc with my destiny. He held up that radar gun, pulled the trigger, and changed my world. Gosh, I wish I could remember his name so I could thank him.

As I told you earlier, my route was the longest one. Generally, most of the drivers were gone by the time I returned to the barn. Not this night, though. They were all there. Each of them fancied himself a real Don Rickles or Alan King.

"So, Parnelli Jones, which gear were you in when he slapped the gun on you?"

"If I hadn't seen it with my own two eyes, I wouldn't have believed it."

"Are you sure Allen Funt wasn't somewhere and you were on Candid Camera?"

I took it all in stride, but I was concerned about whether or not the school district would let me continue driving the bus for the last three to four weeks of the school year. Fortunately, my traffic court date wasn't until early June. School was out before I was officially found guilty of doing thirty-seven in a twenty-five mile per hour zone.

I would guess it was about four weeks before I got the letter. When I saw the Cedar Falls School District logo on the envelope, I was pretty certain I knew what it was.

Dear Mr. Pratt,
During a routine search of your driving record it was determined you have recently been found guilty of a moving violation for speeding. The safety of our students is our first priority and district policy requires us to rescind our offer of employment to you for the upcoming school year.... Blah, blah, blah.

Did I mention my girlfriend for most of the previous three years had recently told me I wasn't Mr. Right? A good portion of that summer was spent drowning my sorrows with my buddy Scott (aka Gilbert), he too having been discarded by his first love. Scott's mother admonished us for feeling sorry for ourselves. She sought to shame us out of our depression by delivering what I consider to be the most memorable put down of my life.

"You guys are pathetic. Look at yourselves. Here you are, two twenty year olds... you are at the height of your sexual capacity. You have all that lead in your pencils and no one to write to.
I repeat myself, you are pathetic." Shirlee was one of a kind. I still smile every time I think of her.

It just so happened I received the reject letter from the school district on a Monday as I was about to head off to barbershop chorus practice. By now everyone in our extended family had heard the story of how Tim had been stopped for speeding while driving a school bus filled with five-year-olds. Most were confident I would not be driving a school bus in the near future, so it was no shock to my Uncle Vern when I confirmed this suspicion at chorus rehearsal.

The chorus was working on Bobby Vinton's *Melody of Love*. (Bobby Vinton is Polish and at times has been referenced as the Polish Prince). They were learning one of the verses in Polish to impress their hosts when they went to Poland.

"*O moja droga ja cie kocham*, means that I love you so. *Moja droga ja cie kocham*, more than you'll ever know..." It was a catchy little tune. " So, that's what Polish sounds like," I thought.

Then Uncle Vern repeated his offer to lend me the money if I wanted to go to Poland. All of a sudden it hit me. Why not? Clearly the bus driving gods didn't want me to drive a bus. Cupid had seen fit to direct his arrow away from me. I had a chance to visit a communist country. I had never been on a plane, and my uncle was making me an offer that was hard to refuse. I decided to accept Uncle Vern's offer. I was going to Poland.

Chapter 2: Poland

About twenty of the seventy-five chorus members had signed up for the trip. In addition, there were probably ten wives accompanying their husbands. It was mid-August, 1975, and I remember it was decided we would wear our casual show outfits to the airport so we could easily be identified as a group. You see, barbershoppers are not shy about singing. They need almost no provocation to break out in song. They will sing in restaurants, on airplanes, in subways, (we didn't have any of those in Des Moines), and even in the men's room. All that is required is a pitch pipe, a lead, a tenor, a baritone, and a bass. You don't even need to know the other singers because every barbershopper knows a series of ten to twelve songs referred to as "Polecat" songs. I think the group thought if we all wore the show outfits it might lead to more opportunities to sing during the trip. Surely, some stewardess or passenger would notice we were all wearing the same hideous outfits and ask who we were. Rather than answer the question, we would blow a pitch pipe and belt out *Down Our Way*.

I told you the outfits were hideous, didn't I? Picture this: Red and white checkerboard shirts, navy blue leisure suits, white belts, and white patent leather boots. No joke. We had purchased those outfits earlier that year because the Grand Finale to our annual show had been a tribute to the USA, where we sang *You're a Grand Old Flag* while executing some elaborate spiral maneuver one of our chorus members, Burdette Thompson, had choreographed. We reasoned the next year was to be our nation's bicentennial and the red, white, and blue theme would eliminate the need for a different outfit for a couple of years.

I am no slave to fashion, to which my wife and children will vigorously attest, but even I know if one is "vertically challenged" and "girth enhanced" (apt descriptors of a fair number of DeMoinaires at the time) the last things you want to draw attention to are your expanding waistline and your absence of height. But there we were with those white belts, plaid shirts, and white boots. From a distance our outfits would have made Stan Laurel look like Oliver Hardy. We didn't care. We were off to do our part to promote international understanding via song. But first, we had to stop in New York City.

We went to New York City for one day to be prepped on some of the dos and don'ts during our trip, and to get a crash course in Polish daily life. There were more *don'ts* than *dos*.

"Don't wander away from the group during daily tours."
"Don't talk politics unless someone initiates the topic."
"Do ask permission before taking a photo of anything military."
"Above all, don't... I repeat, *do not* change money on the street."

We also went to the Polish Embassy for an official reception with the Ambassador.

While in New York we were joined by a makeshift soccer team comprised of players from two colleges: Davis-Elkins College in West Virginia and Towson University located near Baltimore, Maryland. This team would be traveling with us on the same flights to and from Poland, but would have a different itinerary. While we were introducing Poles to that favorite American pastime of barbershop quartet music, the soccer players were to promote international understanding by allowing Polish club teams to drub them in soccer matches.

I think the soccer players were quite good, but they were thrown together with no practice time and were asked to play club teams of men three to four years older. I felt an immediate kinship with the guys on the soccer team, primarily because they were my age. Every person with the DeMoinaires delegation was at least ten years my senior.

I remember wandering Manhattan with four or five of the DeMoinaires for a few hours. We went to Times Square, identified the Empire State Building, and stopped at some nice restaurant for a big steak. I even took a few tugs of a cigar when Barney Alleman offered it.

On the walk back to the Waldorf Astoria Hotel to retire for the evening I wasn't even worried about getting lost. All I had to do was ask someone if they had seen anyone wearing the same clothes I was wearing.

Roger Spahr was my roommate on this trip. He was the current chapter president for the DeMoinaires and among the closest to me in age. His wife, Sonie, did not make the trip. Roger had had some health problems earlier that year, and he was big into fitness at the time. He was running several miles a day, eating a very strict diet, and had begun regulating his metabolism to adjust to Polish time for the week leading up to our departure. Consequently, he wasn't with the group which dined on the steaks and smoked the cigars because he had gone to bed at 6:00 PM. He got up and went running the next morning around 2:00 AM. When I woke up, he told me some hooker had propositioned him right outside the hotel lobby at about 3:00 AM. It's amazing what little details one remembers after thirty plus years.

The only thing I remember from the flight out of JFK to Warsaw was my Uncle Vern and Aunt LaVanche standing up as we were taxiing down the runway to say, "Has anyone seen Tim? Is Tim on the plane? Where is he?"

I was twenty years old. This was the trip of a lifetime. There was no way I was going to miss this trip. I was seated two rows behind them, but now everyone on the plane knew who Tim was and that his aunt and uncle were on the plane, too. I was simultaneously embarrassed, angry, and appreciative.

It was approaching 6:00 AM when we arrived in Warsaw. We were met by a young lady about my age, who spoke fluent English. She identified herself as our tour guide for the next few weeks. Her name was Maria Wołowska (Vo-wof-ska). I thought she was cute. There was another girl with her who asked the soccer players to identify themselves and to follow her, because they would be staying at a different hotel. I didn't catch her name but she also was about my age, and kind of cute.

She was obviously their tour guide. To that point in my life all I knew of East European women was the East German Women's Olympic Swim Team. Clearly, that paradigm was shifting.

Since we arrived early in the morning, we were scheduled for a full day of sightseeing in Warsaw. We went to Łazienki (Wah-zhen-kee) Park where we decided to pay homage to the great Polish composer, Fryderyk Chopin, by giving an impromptu barbershop concert at the base of his monument, one of the most famous of Polish landmarks. There were mixed reviews of our efforts. Apparently, in 1975 Warsaw, any concert at Łazienki required prior consent from somebody, because an official-looking uniformed man came by to tell us we could not sing there. Maria took up our cause, and a rather heated discussion in Polish ensued. We didn't need to speak the native language to know it would be best if we stopped singing.

We were barely five hours into our visit and we had already been to the brink of an international incident. The *Enculturation* guy in New York had failed to include "Don't sing in revered public places" in that list of dos and don'ts. By golly, we were barbershoppers. We were intending to spread goodwill via song wherever we went. The Poles were supposed to listen and enjoy. They must not have gotten that memo.

The day's tour concluded with a trip to the Old Market Square where we viewed a stirring film of the Nazi destruction of Warsaw. The Germans had vowed to raze Warsaw to the ground as they were retreating toward the end of The War. They even recorded for posterity their efforts to do so while, it is said, the Russians allowed it to happen waiting just across the Vistula River. In a tribute to the resilience of the Polish spirit, the Poles rebuilt the Old Market Square exactly as it had been prior to its destruction.

We were given about an hour to explore the square with instructions to meet at the bus promptly at 4:00 PM, when we would return to our hotel. Maria and Małgosia (a second guide assigned to us for the city of

Warsaw tour) took a head count at 4:00 PM, only to discover we were two people short. It was quickly determined our two missing people were my Uncle Vern and Aunt LaVanche. I couldn't help myself. I stood up on the bus, much as they had done on the JFK runway, and said, "Has anyone seen Vern and LaVanche?"

The bus erupted in laughter, easing the tension. After twenty minutes of searching the entire square we left for the hotel, sans Vern and LaVanche. All of us were a little concerned, yet somewhat amused. Surely they would make their way back to the hotel, wouldn't they? I confess to a sense of mild relief when we discovered they had returned to the hotel, via what I am certain was a far-too-expensive taxi, after having lost their way in the Old Market Square. I was as much relieved for Maria as I was for Vern and LaVanche. Losing two Americans probably wouldn't have looked good on her job evaluation.

Roger was the administrative head of our group for this trip. We sat at Maria's table for the evening meal so the two of them could review the next day's schedule. Included in the itinerary was some afternoon free time where we might have a chance to recover from jet lag. We also had the option of going to watch the soccer team play its first match, something I wanted to do.

During evening supper, a lighter meal in Poland, I asked Maria, "So what does the tour guide do when the tour is done for the day? What do young Poles do for evening entertainment?"

To my surprise she said, "Well, it isn't on the schedule, but we can go out for a late dinner or to a club if you like. I am the tour guide and part of my job is to help you experience Poland."

I was all for that. Most of our group was dead tired having lost six hours in the time change. Honestly, I was pretty tired, too, but here was a chance to go out with a girl on my first night in Poland. Remember, Roger was not tired because he had been preparing for the time change.

The three of us agreed to meet at about 9:00 PM to go to wherever Maria suggested.

We went to the top of the Grand Hotel. It was much closer to the center of Warsaw and was an older hotel. I could tell it was a nice hotel, but I had little to compare it to in Poland or the US. It's not like I was among the globetrotting elite. I was an ex-bus driver college kid from Iowa. We were escorted to a table not far from the orchestra. I call it an orchestra rather than a band because there must have been at least ten instrumentalists and a singer.

My experience with bars and clubs to that point had been pretty much limited to Poor Richard's Lounge, the local watering hole where we drank beer and shot pool. And to Uncle Sam's, the hot disco where we paid a two dollar cover, drank "Firecrackers" and discoed, bumped, and sang along to the Bee Gees, Elton John, and the Doobie Brothers. This place wasn't like either of those places, but I loved it.

We ordered a light meal and some wine. Roger and I took turns dancing with Maria. She was a very good dancer, very light on her feet. I have always been amazed at how women can be so good at following on the dance floor. We had engaging conversation, good food, fine wine, and attractive company. If Maria's job was to send us home to America with good impressions of Poland, she was certainly doing her job well. It was after 1:00 AM when we returned to the hotel. I was beginning to think this was going to be a nice trip.

Until the day that we left New York, I had never heard the term, "Black Market." Even after it was explained to me, I was unclear about what it meant or why it existed. But at breakfast the next morning, I was to get a crash course in underground economics. One of the older guys in our group, John Abrams, pulled me aside and said he just exchanged money with our bus driver, George, (Jerzy) and got ninety złotys for one dollar. That fact is irrelevant unless you know our "official" exchange rate was thirty-three złotys per dollar, and we had been required to exchange ten dollars per day at nineteen złotys per dollar in order to get our visas.

For the most part, I am one who follows the rules. When an authority figure says, "Do not change money on the street," I plan on following directions. But here was John, swearing George's offer was legitimate, and he would exchange money at this rate with anyone who wanted to trade. He showed me the money. I resisted the temptation to exchange money until Mike Rehberg told me he had done the same thing. Mike was our chorus director and in real life was the head of the crime lab for the Department of Criminal Investigation of Iowa. Heck, if he thought it was okay, that was good enough for me. I exchanged about fifty dollars at ninety złotys per dollar.

I already thought dinner the previous evening had been very reasonable—almost cheap—for the type of place where we dined. I think the total cost including the wine had been about fifty zł per person. If I went back to the Grand Hotel this evening and had dinner and drinks, I wasn't even going to spend a dollar! I could pick up the tab for all three of us and still not spend three dollars. What little I had learned of communism in Mr. Geery's economics class at Saydel High School hadn't included this little perk. I was rich. Man, was I going to enjoy the next two weeks.

While on the bus traveling to the soccer match I was talking with Maria about how much fun I had the night before. I told her it sure would be nice if we could find another person to go with us if we would have a chance to go out again. Specifically, I asked if she knew the other girl at the airport—the one with the soccer team. I figured she probably did, but I was not expecting her response.

"Well, as a matter of fact I do know her. Her name is Ewa, and we attend the university together. She is my roommate there."

"Do you think she would like to go with us tonight, if we were to go back to the same place?" I asked.

"I don't know, but I will ask her when we get to the match."

When we arrived at the soccer match I was introduced to Ewa. (In Polish "w" is pronounced like a "v" and the "e" is like the word "ever"). I remember it was a warm day, and Ewa was wearing a pair of large sunglasses, white jeans, and a Davis Elkins College tee shirt. And she was smoking.

If you have been abroad, then you probably know it is not uncommon for Europeans to smoke. Oh, who am I kidding, in 1975, rare was the Pole who didn't smoke! Maria smoked. George smoked. The uniformed guard at Łazienki Park smoked. I'll bet Chopin himself probably smoked if it was available in his day. It was one of the very first things we had noticed within hours of landing in Warsaw. So, it was not unusual to see Ewa smoke.

After a brief introduction, Ewa and Maria had a conversation in Polish which concluded in English with Maria saying, "She will join us tonight at the Grand Hotel, but it will be late. She can't leave until she is finished with her formal duties with the team. It will be about 10:00 PM before she can meet us there."

I think the Americans lost the soccer match, 1-0.

Roger, Maria, and I were waiting in the lobby of the Grand Hotel at 10:00 PM. At about 10:15 PM a huge tour bus pulled up to the building and opened its door. I could see there was but one passenger on the bus. It was Ewa. As she exited the bus she said something to the driver and he drove away. I guess when you are in charge of the tour, the driver does whatever you tell him to do. Why pay for a taxi when you have a bus at your personal disposal? We went inside and had a wonderful meal, great conversation, and danced to the orchestra once again. This time, however, poor Maria was given a reprieve from the dance floor, courtesy of Ewa's willingness to accept my repeated invitations to fox trot.

We didn't leave until about 2:00 AM. The door man flagged down a nearby taxi for Ewa. I gave Ewa a handful of złotys for cab fare and startled her by kissing her goodnight, smack on the lips. To this day, Ewa tells everyone she was shocked, and I could tell she was, but I was even more shocked by my own initiative. There was just something about being in a foreign country, thousands of miles from home, as the only single guy on the tour, and with more money than I had ever had, which caused all inhibitions to dissipate.

I like to think that even as a youngster I was pretty good at picking up on the non-verbal cues people would send out. Sometimes I misinterpret these cues, but for the most part I would include this skill among my very limited talents. But this skill was not really required at breakfast the next morning to determine some of the wives in our group thought Roger had committed some unpardonable sin, and Maria was a bit of a hussy. Sonie was home in Ankeny tending to two young boys and here was her husband, out to the wee hours of the morning with some young chippy. The one saving grace was that Tim had been with them, too.

I sensed somehow most of our party was living vicariously through me and were happy I had gone out after hours with the tour guides. Roger was not afforded the same sentiment. I don't know what those women thought Roger was going to do. After all, Roger's father was also a barbershopper and his parents were on the trip! Besides, Sonie has the biggest brown eyes you have ever seen, and my sister was their babysitter. No, Roger was enjoying the experience, but not too much. I think Roger was almost reveling in the commotion he was creating.

After a day trip to Żelazowa Wola (Chopin's birthplace), our group and the soccer team were headed in different directions. We were off to Poznań, and the soccer team was headed for Łódź. We wouldn't be back together until the city of Kraków, about a week later.

Poznań is the home of Adam Mickiewicz University. It boasts the finest program for the study of the English language in all of Poland. Of greater interest to me, however, was that this was where Ewa and Maria went to school. Surely, Maria had other female friends in this town. We toured Poznań and the nearby town of Gniezno, where we saw ruins of a church dating to the tenth century. We visited Rogalin and saw thousand-year-old trees. We sang a concert at a hospital. I had a brief solo. We went to dinner and a show, as the entire group, at the Adria Restaurant. Maria was anticipating my request. Yes, her friend, Lidka, would love to join our group for the evening. Was this a great country, or what?!

Let me tell you all that was included with dinner and a show at the Adria Restaurant. Dinner was, well, dinner. I had duck. But the show was a little more than most of the DeMoinaires had envisioned. In addition to the band and singer there was a comedian (at least that is what I deduced, since all of the Poles in the restaurant were laughing hysterically) and a couple who performed a contemporary dance. The final act was a striptease. This was not the raunchy bumping and grinding of a totally nude woman entwined with a chrome pole, but more like what I suspect was a titillating early Gypsy Rose Lee routine. Only after her gloves and outer skirt came off did I awaken to the fact this woman was stripping. It was tasteful, if one can describe publicly removing one's clothes as tasteful, but there was still something very odd about this performance. What was it? I could look around the room and see others in our group with similar looks on their faces. There was just something not quite right. And then it hit me, at almost the same instant it hit several others. It was the music. Where had I heard that song before? As barbershoppers will sometimes do, some of us began to quietly hum and harmonize with the music while this woman removed another piece of clothing. What was that song? Da dee da dee da dee dum…boom, crash… Da dee da dee da dee du uh um… Oh my God, this woman was stripping to *Just a Closer Walk With Thee*! This was one of the hymns our chorus sang when we performed our religious set at Des Moines area churches in the summer. It was all we could do to keep ourselves from breaking out in full song as she reached the breast-bearing climax to her number.

Following the show most of the group headed back to our hotel, which was really just one of the college dorms, but some of us stayed to dance the night away. Included in the group that stayed was Lidka.

Have you ever been on a date or been dancing with someone who speaks not one word of English? Neither had I. I was whispering sweet nothings into her ear all night knowing full well she had no clue what I was saying. We enjoyed the evening so much we agreed to do it again the next evening. I have no idea if the girl really enjoyed my company, or was doing Maria a favor, or just liked to be treated to a fine meal complete with dancing, but I know I had a great time.

The next day was a grueling fourteen hour bus trip from Poznań to Kraków. Once again our accommodations were in *Międzynarodowy Hotel Studencki* (International Students' Hotel). This was a college dormitory where students from all around the world stayed during their studies in Kraków. A few of the women complained to each other they didn't appreciate the suite arrangement where two dorm rooms shared a bathroom. I thought the place was fine, but then again, I was a college kid having the time of his life. I would have been happy with a pup tent and an outhouse. I had money. I had learned a half-dozen words in Polish, and now I needed to find a date.

Kraków is a beautiful city. For the most part, it was left unscathed by the destruction of World War II, even though it was the sight of one of the many Jewish ghettos. It is the home of Jagiellonian University, which was founded in 1364. The great astronomer, Copernicus, who taught us the sun—not the Earth—is the center of our solar system, studied at Jagiellonian. (Both of my children would study at this university in separate summers more than thirty years after my first visit to Kraków). Wawel Castle, where the great kings of Poland are entombed, dominates the city from a hill near the center of town. The Market Square rivals some of the great squares of Europe. Karol Wojtyła was Archbishop here before becoming Pope John Paul II. In nearby Wieliczka is a huge salt mine, a must-see for anyone traveling to Kraków. The quaint mountain resort town of Zakopane is easily accessible from Kraków. So, too, is that reminder to us all of man's capacity for evil—Oświęcim (Auschwitz). If but one city can be on your Poland itinerary, you would be well-advised to make it Kraków.

We visited each of these places during our stay in Kraków. We sang in the great underground hall at the Salt Mine of Wieliczka. I still get goose bumps when I think of the echo and those acoustics. We sang in the Main Square. We sang in Zakopane. We did not sing at Auschwitz.

Each morning we would go down to the cafeteria of *Międzynarodowy Hotel Studencki* and parade through the line for breakfast. As we selected our food items, there were women on the kitchen side of the counter who were constantly replacing them. Most of the women were my mother's age, but there was one young girl with a very pretty face and a nice smile. Our trip was winding down and I wanted to seize every opportunity to enjoy Polish nightlife. I had never been to Kraków and had no idea if and/or when I would ever return.

During breakfast Maria agreed to go out for late dinner and dancing at the Hotel Cracovia that evening. This conversation was a rather public one and several others in our group asked to join us for the late dinner. Then one of the guys threw down the gauntlet.

"Hey, Tim, did you see that cute girl in the cafeteria line? Why don't you ask her to join us tonight?"

By this point in our trip everyone was having fun knowing that I was having fun. They wanted to see if I really had the chest hair to go ask the girl to join me for dinner. Like I told you earlier, all inhibitions were gone. I walked up to the cafeteria line, smiled at this girl, and uttered all of the Polish I knew:

"Dzień dobry, Pani." ("Good day, Miss").

From then on it was sign language, smiles, and stick figures drawn on a napkin.

"You and me (while simultaneously pointing to her and myself), go dancing (here I struck my best Fred Astaire pose) Hotel Cracovia (fortunately this was the same in English and Polish) 9:00 PM? (here I wrote 9:00 PM on the napkin and pointed at my watch)."

Now that I had already put the mechanics together once, I repeated everything in just the same way a second time, as if it would be clearer because I had synchronized the gestures with the disjointed English. I have to tell you, this was quite a scene. All of the older Polish ladies came out from the kitchen and were laughing and speaking to her in Polish. The poor girl turned beet red—but she was smiling. I looked back at the table where our group was sitting and they were hanging on every word, too. Did she understand what I was asking? Would she turn me down? I hadn't felt this much pressure since high school when I asked Linda Reese to go to the *Summer of '42* with me (Linda only said yes after the third time, just to get me to quit calling her). With the tension building to a crescendo, she nodded her head, yes. The kitchen ladies clapped their hands with approval. Mission accomplished. I had a date.

I hustled back to our table and asked Maria to confirm departure times and other logistics with this girl. Oh yeah, and could she ask the girl, her name? Her name was Maria, too. It was Maria Dec ("dets"). Many times I have wondered what ever happened to her. She went out that night with us and even came on our tour the next day to a beautiful castle near Kraków, known as Pieskowa Skala. (Apparently the Poles did not require liability waivers for non-official tour members and the tour guide's authority extended well beyond personal use of the bus).

A few pages ago, I asked if you have ever been on a date with someone who spoke absolutely no English. Now, in less than a week I had done it twice. I was beginning to think maybe the girls liked me better when they couldn't understand me. But communication was not going to be a problem for my last evening in town, because the soccer boys were now in Kraków, and so, too, was their tour guide. She had no problems with my native language.

We had a final night in Kraków before we would return to Warsaw and then depart for home. Both of the tour groups went out together for a farewell dinner at the Hotel Cracovia. We would have one more night in Warsaw, but it was reserved for packing, not partying. I don't remember a lot about the last evening in Kraków, although I did manage a dance or two with Ewa. Appropriately so, she was tending to her guide responsibilities with the soccer team.

September 1st is a solemn occasion in Poland. It is a day of remembrance. On that day in 1939, Adolf Hitler and the German Army introduced Poland to the "blitzkrieg," marking the beginning of World War II. Less than twelve months earlier British Prime Minister Neville Chamberlain naively announced he had secured "peace for our time" when he agreed to Germany's acquisition of the Sudetenland, a region of Czechoslovakia inhabited by a large number of Germans. Hitler's stated reason for the attack on Poland was because of Poland's refusal to allow Germany access to the "free city" of Gdańsk, (known by the Germans as Danzig) located on the Baltic Sea. Though it was completely inside of Poland, Gdańsk/Danzig had been declared a "free city" under the Treaty of Versailles. A dispute arose over the governance of the city. While "appeasement" may have been Chamberlain's favored form of diplomacy, it was not shared by the Poles. Hitler responded militarily.

September 1st was our final day in Poland that summer. We went to the Old Market Square and were given some free time to shop for souvenirs, or to get a shave and a haircut. That's what Roger did.

The year 1975 was the one hundredth anniversary of the founding of Ankeny, Iowa, a Des Moines suburb and Roger's hometown. Like many communities, Ankeny held a variety of festivals, complete with different contests to commemorate its centennial year. One of those contests was the "best beard" contest. Roger did not shave for more than a year leading up to the event in July of 1975. I don't know how he placed in the contest, but I can tell you his beard was a good five or six inches below his chin when we left for Poland. One might have thought Roger would have removed his beard prior to our departure, since the beard contest had concluded a few weeks earlier. But Roger had his passport photo taken while he had his beard. He was worried that if he shaved before the trip, his appearance would be so different from his passport photo that it might invite some unnecessary attention from airport officials.

Apparently, on that final day in Warsaw, Roger had decided to risk misidentification and any subsequent consequences. He told me he was going to shave his beard and asked Maria to direct him to the "*fryzjer*" (barber) in the Old Market. I left him at the door and we agreed I would return in an hour, when we would head back to our hotel for the final time. When I returned to the "*fryzjer*," Roger was nowhere to be found. At first, I assumed he was in some nearby shop, but after several minutes of searching with no luck, I began to get worried. I found Maria and asked her if she had seen Roger. Before she could respond, the man standing less than five feet away from me said, "Hey, I'm right here."

I had walked past this man several times in my search for Roger. I recognized the voice and he was speaking English, but I honestly did not know it was Roger. I have never seen a person's appearance change so dramatically in less than an hour, than Roger Spahr's appearance changed that day. Not one person in our group knew who he was when we returned to the hotel.

At the airport the next day we all said our final goodbyes. We took pictures. We gave flowers to Maria. I sought out Ewa to exchange addresses with her, too. I even gave her another kiss, but this one was on the cheek. I made Ewa and Maria promise to write, and I told them to come and visit Iowa some day. I was truly melancholy, if not downright sad, on the long flight home. I remember thinking to myself, "I cannot believe this is the last time I will ever see these people and this country."

Chapter 3: Letter Writing

As I recall, there was a fair number of family and friends to greet us at the Des Moines Airport. The DeMoinaires were tired. We didn't even sing. I had to unpack, wash clothes, and pack again to leave the next day for Cedar Falls to start my junior year of college. (Note: I did NOT take the leisure suit, checkerboard shirt, white boots or white belt with me). School had already been in session for a week, so it was important for me to leave as quickly as possible. I was excited to be starting a new university in a different city, but I was preoccupied with the trip that had just concluded.

On the drive home from the airport I learned that, simultaneous to Roger's shave and haircut in Warsaw, there had been a massive explosion in Des Moines caused by the derailment of several train cars carrying some sort of toxic chemical. (I doubt any other person who may have been aware of these two events has ever thought of them as occurring at the same time, but that's just how my mind works). My parents had agreed to house some guests of a nearby hotel who had been evacuated. I had a lot to report, but so, too, did my family. I think they sensed I had really enjoyed my trip to the other side of the world, but things were pretty hectic for that brief time before my departure for Cedar Falls.

The elevators were out when I arrived at Bender Hall. I thought to myself this was God's way of telling me I was wrong to drive over the speed limit when transporting young children. Fortunately, I had brought with me only the bare necessities of a couple of suitcases filled with clothes, a lamp, and some toiletries. I got everything transported in just two trips up the stairs—all eleven flights of them. The room I had been assigned was 1109 Bender Hall, a place I would come to know as the single coldest place in all of Iowa. There is probably some irony in the fact my new roomie was himself rather cold, but again I digress.

I could count on one hand the number of times I had visited the Grand View College Library during my first two years of higher education. I had been on campus less than two hours when I asked directions to the University of Northern Iowa (UNI) Library. Having been previously exposed to the Dewey Decimal System as a methodology for categorizing literary works, I needed no help in locating the book on learning Polish. Notice I said *the book*, not the plural form, *books*, but rather the singular noun, *book*. At least I didn't have to waste time in the selection process.

Using my newly-acquired student ID I checked out my one book with the librarian. He said I should study hard because the book was due in three weeks. The slip on the inside cover where he stamped the return date had no prior stamps in it. There was only the identifier, "Property of Iowa State Teacher's College," the pre-1967 name of the university. Since its acquisition by the university this book had never been checked out. I faithfully renewed the book for checkout every three weeks during the first semester. Finally, during the second semester the librarian called me to say I could use the book for as long as I was a student at UNI, or until someone came in to request it. Had I not rescued this book, I am certain it was destined to travel no further than the reference section of that library. It was a valuable communication tool for me.

Immediately upon arrival in Cedar Falls I began corresponding with each of the four women whom I had met in Poland. Two of them, Maria and Ewa, were fluent in English, while the other two, Maria Dec and Lidka Piwko, were not. I was trying to teach myself Polish from this book. I studied it more than any of my course work—except Football Theory. I loved that class. When I would write to Lidka and Maria Dec, I simply plagiarized whole sentences from the conversations in the book. I am certain both girls found it odd I would include some phrase like, "I am going inside to warm up because it is so cold out here," or "The library is straight ahead and I am going there, now," into my letters, but they were probably equally impressed I wrote them in flawless Polish. Predictably so, I received maybe one or two letters from Maria Dec and

Lidka Piwko, and our correspondence discontinued after a few months. Such was not the case with the other two, especially Ewa.

My brother's fiancée, Laura, was an outstanding artist. During that time right after Thanksgiving dinner, when the men are fighting to stay awake while watching the Detroit Lions disappoint their fans yet again, Laura asked me what I wanted for Christmas. I asked if she would design four personalized Christmas cards which I could send to Poland. I gave her the words, *"Wesołych Świąt i Szczęśliwego Nowego Roku!"* (Merry Christmas and Happy New Year) to include with each of the four cards. I felt really bad when she presented me with four of the prettiest Christmas cards I had ever seen. I really didn't mean for her to go to all that trouble, but they were very nice cards.

By the time the New Year rolled around I had noticed a correspondence pattern emerging. I would write a letter to Maria, wait a couple of weeks, write another one, wait a couple of weeks and maybe get a reply. I would write a letter to Ewa, get a reply in about two weeks, write another letter to Ewa, and get another reply in two weeks. Hmm... I found I liked receiving letters as much as I liked sending them. Maybe more. I still remember the dorm name (*Jagienka*) and the street name (*Obornicka*) in Poznań, Poland. Since Ewa and Maria lived together, I was pretty certain they were sharing the contents of my letters with each other. I really didn't need to duplicate my efforts. There wasn't anything too personal or intimate in them, anyway. So, I decided to direct most of my letters to the one who was reciprocating my efforts. And remember, she was cute.

School was going pretty well at UNI, though I had little free time. I was taking two evening classes and a total of twenty credit hours for the semester. I did all of this with no classes on Friday. My last class for the week (the Football Theory class I referenced earlier) ended at noon on Thursday. I did this because my father had helped me to get a job in Des Moines on Fridays and Saturdays, yet another consequence of not landing the bus-driving job in Cedar Falls.

I was to wash all of the trucks for Churchill Freight Lines over the weekend. I usually worked on Friday nights and most of the day on Saturday. Occasionally, I would load and unload freight at the Churchill freight dock on Friday during the day. I drove back to Des Moines every Thursday afternoon and returned to school every Sunday night. Somehow I did manage to drink my fair share of beer and bond with the guys on my floor that semester, but the highlight of my week was going to my mailbox on the first floor of Bender Hall and seeing a letter with brightly colored stamps from Poland.

I think it was early February when Ewa wrote in a letter that she had saved the money for a trip to the US. She had never been to the "West" and would really like to visit, but, in order to apply for a passport, she needed a formal invitation from someone outside of the Eastern Bloc. *If* she was granted a passport by the Polish authorities, she could *then* request a visa from the US Embassy. Neither of these items was a certainty. By contrast, the summer before, I hadn't even made the decision to travel to Poland until four weeks before the trip. I took a couple of pictures, filled out the application, sent in fifteen dollars, and had a passport in two weeks. It didn't work that way in Poland. I knew nothing of this process, but if Ewa wanted to come and visit the US, I was going to do what I could to help make it happen.

I quickly learned an invitation can only be sent by adults who are not claimed as dependents on someone else's tax return. That ruled me out. So, while at home the following weekend I asked Mom and Dad if they would issue the invitation. They discussed it and thought it would be kind of interesting to have a "foreign exchange student" for the summer. They sent Ewa a formal invitation.

Ewa received the invitation and was granted a passport. She now needed a visa from the US Embassy. To obtain a visa, Ewa had to prove she would not become a financial burden to the US. My parents had to complete an Affidavit of Support, which was a very detailed summary of income, assets, liabilities, etc. Ewa then traveled to Warsaw for her interview with the US Embassy.

In early May, I received a letter from Ewa saying she had been granted a visa to the US and was coming to the United States on June 20th. I wasn't certain what to expect, but Marv and Scott (Whitey and Gilbert) didn't have pretty twenty-one year old females moving in with their parents for the summer. This was going to be an interesting three months.

Chapter 4: The Summer of 1976

Once I learned Ewa would be first arriving in Chicago, Mom thought it would be best if she was met there by Aunt Lucille (Mom's sister) and Uncle Clif. They were planning to come to Des Moines for my brother's wedding the next week, anyway. Ewa could rest at their place and ride with them to Des Moines. I wasn't so sure that was a good idea; not because my Aunt and Uncle weren't good people—two more hospitable people have never been born. It was more the other stuff. Like, Clif always had an off-color joke, or one that was politically incorrect. I had visions of him greeting Ewa and then immediately asking her, "Do you know why Polacks never use ice in their drinks? Because they lost the recipe." This would be followed by a big laugh which would cause everyone else to laugh, even if they didn't want to. Then Lucille would admonish Clif, and this would start a running verbal tête-à-tête lasting until everyone went to bed.

Mom was insistent, so I just had to trust Clif and Lucille's warmth and generosity, not their constant sparring, would influence Ewa's first impression of America. I later discovered any fears I had were completely misplaced. Clif and Lucille Gourley would go on to host several Poles for their first nights in America. In fact, many in Poland today believe the official US point of entry in Chicago is actually a little condo at 232 Frederick Place in Wood Dale, Illinois.

I must have been working when Ewa first arrived with Clif and Lucille because I have no recollection of that event. As we ate dinner that evening, it became obvious that Ewa and my parents were going to get along just fine. My parents had heard a lot about Ewa. They were excited to have her. They just weren't real certain as to the nature of their son's relationship with this girl. They weren't certain because if their son knew (which he did not), he wasn't talking about it.

My two best buddies, Marv and Scott, had been anxious to meet this girl, too. Even though we went to three different universities that year,

(Scott to Iowa State in Ames, Marv to Drake University in Des Moines and me to UNI), we had managed to stay in close contact. They stopped by to meet Ewa. I was mortified when, after Scott was introduced to Ewa, he uttered one of the most offensive of Polish expletives.

You see, earlier in the school year I had visited Scott at Iowa State and discovered there were some Polish students from Warsaw Polytechnic attending ISU in a study abroad program. I met with them, showed them photos of my trip, (they even recognized one of their professors who was in the background of a photo I had taken in the Old Market in Warsaw), and told them of my interest in learning the language. Before we went out for a night of bar hopping to further the international peace process, they saw fit to teach me every swear word in the Polish language. They made me repeat the words until I sounded like a native speaker. Throughout the evening, between pitchers of beer, they would give me a swear word in English and I would have to repeat the Polish equivalent. I am certain it was not nearly as funny as we all thought it was, but they confirmed I could swear with the best of them in Polish. Of course, Marv and Scott had asked me to teach them a few of the words, too. So, when Scott met Ewa, he threw out one of the few Polish words he knew. I quickly explained how it was Scott even knew such words. Fortunately, Ewa let it pass without comment.

Yes, I was living with Mom and Dad during that summer. My sister, Kristi, had her room, Mom and Dad had their room, and Ewa got my room. I was moved to the basement. My brother, Steve, was moving to his fiancée's home. Is it a date if she asks to be picked up at 7:00 PM, and to be prompt, you start up the stairs at 6:59? Or when you drop her off at the end of the evening it's in your own garage? Or when you both prepare for your date in the same bathroom? Today this happens all the time, as many young couples live together. But we weren't *living together*; we were just "living together," if that makes sense. Well, at least I had no problems finding her house.

Just one week after Ewa arrived, on June 26th, 1976, my brother was married to Laura. I was the best man and Laura's two sons were the groomsmen while a friend of Laura's, Laura's daughter, and my sister stood up for her. Our family really liked Laura. She was older than my brother and came with a readymade family, but we genuinely liked Laura and her kids. The wedding was at Central Lutheran Church, followed by a reception at Adventureland Inn.

As you might imagine, relatives came from all over the country for this wedding. Aunts, uncles and cousins came from Chicago, San Diego, Minnesota and various points in Iowa. Of course, the wedding nuptials were the featured attraction, but there was a subplot provoking interest, too. Who was this girl from Poland? Why was she here? How long would she stay? Is she Tim's girlfriend? My poor mother and sister could only answer some of the questions.

"Her name is Ewa, pronounce the *w* like a *v*. She was a tour guide on the trip Tim took to Poland last year. Bill and I invited her to stay with us for three months. I have no idea if she is Tim's girlfriend. We are driving to California for two weeks, and she is going with us. Tim can't go. He has to work. We are leaving on Monday and taking Steve's car. He and Laura are flying to Hawaii for their honeymoon, and will return to San Diego where we will meet them. They will return by car, and we will fly to San Francisco for the International Barbershop Quartet Contest and then fly home."

Mom repeated some version of that story dozens of times at the wedding reception.

Mom, Dad, and Ewa drove to San Diego, California, to leave the car for Steve and Laura, and to visit several relatives in the area. I am certain for Ewa it was more about the journey rather than the destination, but here was a chance for her to see a big slice of the United States. It was also a chance for my parents to get to know her. They traveled through the mountains of Colorado. They stopped at a motel with a swimming pool, lost a few nickels to a one-armed bandit in Las Vegas, and probably made a stop or two for ice cream along the way.

On the nation's Bicentennial, July 4th, 1976, at Art and Saralynn Hopkey's house in Alpine, California, Steve introduced his new bride to a houseful of our relatives. Mom and Dad introduced Ewa to the same group. She had been here less than two full weeks and had met all of my relatives in Chicago, experienced my brother's wedding, met more relatives at the reception, traveled two thousand miles across six states in a car with my parents, met even more relatives, and witnessed the biggest 4th of July celebration in our country's history. Looking back it appears as if we were covertly grooming her for family membership. We weren't playing fair.

The adventure continued in San Francisco. There were cable cars and visits to Fisherman's Wharf, Ghirardelli Square, and Alcatraz. Of course, there was the International Barbershop Contest, too. We can't forget that. The tour guide had become the tourist. She was finding out how much fun that could be. Me? I was driving an asphalt truck for the City of Des Moines Street Maintenance Department... and anxiously awaiting everyone's return.

There was little time to enjoy much of anything when they all arrived back in Des Moines. My Grandpa Nelson (Mom's father) passed away on July14th. Grandpa was ninety years old. He had come here from Norway at the age of seventeen and carved out a decent life as a farmer in north central Iowa. He married a local school marm, Bertha Scott. My mother was the youngest of their five children.

The funeral was held at St. Olaf Lutheran Church, located a few miles west of Belmond, Iowa.

My parents had been married in the same church on July 15th, 1951. Mom and Dad had to celebrate their twenty-fifth wedding anniversary by burying Grandpa in the cemetery adjacent to the church where they were married. I remember thinking it wasn't right to have to bury your father on any wedding anniversary—especially your Silver Anniversary, but there was little I could do.

Years earlier, my mother had told me that on her wedding day, her maternal grandfather had died, but her parents waited until after the ceremony to tell her. Naturally, many of the same relatives who had been at the wedding, and even the relatives who had been in California for July 4th, were at the funeral. Ewa had met more of my relatives—repeatedly—in three weeks than I had seen in the last three family reunions combined. Our houseguest was no longer the girl from Poland; she was an honorary member of the family.

A wedding, a funeral, the nation's two hundredth birthday... what other elements of our culture could I help Ewa experience? That summer we managed to take in a Major League Baseball game in Kansas City with a side trip to the amusement park, Worlds of Fun. We attended a college football game in Ames. We had a picnic at Saylorville Lake, and I taught Ewa to drive. Then she went to the Iowa State Fair.

I could spend hours telling you of the horse barns, or the Varied Industries Building which always featured the fully functioning water faucet appearing to be suspended in mid air, or the Bill Riley Talent Show, or spelling bees, or cow-chip throwing contests, or the biggest boar competition, or hotdogs on a stick, or wonder bars, or a myriad of other things which lure people to this annual spectacle, but none of these was of primary interest to Ewa. She wanted to go there to see Georgia Governor Jimmy Carter. He was running for President of the United States and was coming to the Iowa State Fair. He liked Iowa because he had had some early success in our state's first-in-the-nation caucuses back in January.

I had to work. Mom had to work. Dad had to work. Kristi had to work. But my cousin, Andy Horner, didn't have to work. He had just returned to Iowa from his home in Idaho, to prepare for another year at

Graceland College in Lamoni, Iowa. He was only going to be in town for two or three days, but as luck would have it, he was available and was also interested in seeing Jimmy Carter at the Iowa State Fair. What follows is hearsay and merely represents events as relayed to me by Andy, but I have every reason to believe his account of that day is fundamentally accurate.

Andy and Ewa went to the State Fair and made their way to the general vicinity where Jimmy Carter was scheduled to speak. A massive crowd had gathered in the area surrounding the stage, with the very large press corps occupying the area closest to the stage. Andy recalls he and Ewa were toward the back of the estimated twenty thousand people. A couple of local dignitaries were droning on in effusive praise of the new Democratic nominee for President of the United States. It was obvious Mr. Carter was very soon to speak. Andy says Ewa wanted to be closer to the stage for a better view. She started to weave in and out of the crowd, at first gently moving people aside as she got closer to the stage.

At some point Andy said, "I just couldn't follow her because it was packed too tightly with people, and I could muster only so many, 'excuse me's, 'pardon me's and 'I'm sorry's, and decided to watch and listen from quite a ways back." A few minutes went by and Jimmy Carter came to the stage accompanied by thunderous applause.

Andy had lost sight of Ewa but knew she was somewhere closer to the stage. As Mr. Carter began his comments, there was a minor commotion somewhere near the front. Andy could see Ewa near to where the distraction was taking place. Just then Mr. Carter spoke into the microphone and asked the press corps to sit down so the people just behind them could see. Yep, you guessed it. It was Ewa who was asking the press corps to move so she could see. If this guy was potentially the next leader of the free world and fate had brought her to this point, then she was going to get as close as she could. That night on the local TV news there was a little segment on Jimmy Carter's speech at the State

Fair. There was even a comment about the press having been asked to sit down to allow people to see. This is the woman I came to know and love.

Ewa was scheduled to return to Poland in the middle of September. I didn't return to Cedar Falls in the fall because at the end of that summer I started my student teaching practicum at Ankeny High School. I was also helping to coach the Ankeny freshmen football team. I remember this because I was decked out in maroon and gold coaching garb for that afternoon's game as I drove Ewa to the airport. The whole family went to the airport to see her off, but I drove separately with Ewa. It was a long, slow, sad drive across town. We had spent a lot of time together that summer. Our relationship had certainly grown into a boyfriend/girlfriend thing. Neither of us was too excited about the uncertainty around when, and if, we would see each other again. Our relationship was not to the point where I was ready to ask this girl to marry me, but I sure as heck wasn't ready for her to leave.

The Ankeny freshmen football team beat Indianola that evening. As a young student teacher/coach I had spotted a major flaw in the Indianola defensive coverage to our "spread" formation. (They were inverting on both sides, leaving the middle of the field wide open). I told Coach Leonard that Jim Womble, our tight end, would walk into the end zone if we simply went to our "pro" set rather than our "spread" and hit him right over the middle. He sent the play in. Indianola double inverted, as I had predicted, and Jim Womble walked into the end zone. I knew I could coach this sport. The coaches and players were impressed. I should have been happier than I was.

Chapter 5: The Big Decision

In December I returned to UNI for my final semester of undergraduate work. I was promptly ordered to take several courses intended to "prepare" me for the student teaching experience—*which I had just completed.* I had to observe classes at Peet Junior High and Price Lab School, so I would be better able to handle the classroom situations I had just encountered. I know, it didn't make sense to me either…but I quickly determined I was on pace to graduate in the spring, and I subscribed to the "don't ask, don't tell" approach to this kind of inconsistency.

My recollection of that final semester is mostly a blur. There was some partying with the guys of Kraschel House (11th floor Bender) and believe it or not, I landed a bus driving gig for Price Lab School to earn some pocket money. Apparently, they didn't care much about my checkered past pursuant to that position.

Randy Skilling and Paul Boisjolie were my best buddies at UNI. When I had last seen them in May, they knew Ewa was coming to stay with my parents for the summer and they were now extremely curious to know just how the summer had gone. I protested I was not the "kiss and tell" type but suggested the summer had gone very well, thank you. It had gone well enough that I was already planning for another trip to Europe.

There was another kid on my floor, John LaFalce, whose father had some diplomatic position in Egypt at the time. At the end of the school year John was planning to fly to Cairo to visit his father. Along the way he was stopping in Paris for a week to see the sights. I was jealous.

I was now exchanging letters almost weekly with Ewa and was trying to figure out how I could get back to Europe. Naturally, I wanted to see Ewa, but I also wanted to see more of Europe. I started to read travel books and gather information about cheap student charter flights, youth hostels, and Eurail passes. I made the decision I was going to Europe as soon as school was out. Now, I had to figure out how to pay for it.

Early in my parents' marriage Dad owned his own truck. He was a self-employed over-the-road-trucker who was a serious candidate for bankruptcy. Ozzie and Harriett never dealt with this problem when raising David and Ricky, but if they had, they could have taken some pointers from Helen and Bill. Dad and Mom had contacted their numerous creditors and made arrangements to pay back every dime owed, even if it was in five or ten dollar monthly increments. It took them a few years to get it done, but every vendor, lender, or service provider was paid in full. I was about to reap the benefit of some of the goodwill they had created.

I went to a banker who was a friend of my father. I asked for a loan-- fifteen hundred dollars—with the first payment due in six months. There was a serious interview.

"Why do you want the money?" "How will you pay it back?" "Do you have a job?" "What collateral do you have?"

My answers were very matter of fact: "To go to Europe." "From my income when I get a teaching job." "No." "None."

After a brief hesitation he announced he was going to "bet on the come" and give me the money. I am certain the fix was in and besides, as I recall Mom and Dad co-signed the note, so the real risk belonged to them. I think Mom and Dad knew exactly what they were doing. I sensed they were comfortable I had internalized some of the values they had preached and lived for the previous twenty years.

My final undergraduate exam (Dr. Ky T. Lee's statistics class) was on a Thursday in early May. The last thing I did before leaving campus was to meet with John LaFalce to determine where we would meet in

Paris three weeks into the future. Neither of us had ever been to Paris. Neither of us spoke French. There were no cell phones, GPSs, or Blackberrys to guide us. We only knew we were arriving on the same day, at different times, and at different airports. We laid out a map of Paris and chose the intersection of Rue something and Rue something else on the Left Bank as our rendezvous point, at exactly 11:00 AM on Monday May 30th. To add to our sense of adventure we agreed to have no contact during those three weeks.

I bought a backpack and then did what all of the travel books advised: 1) lay out the clothes you will need for your trip 2) before packing, get rid of half of them 3) repeat steps one and two 4) pack. I took a pocket knife, which had a variety of attachments, and a collapsible cup. I had a special pouch to wear around my neck where I could keep my passport, plane ticket, and money. I didn't have a credit card. I was not planning to camp, so I didn't need those accessories. I had decided against the Eurail pass because I knew I was going to Poland for at least part of the trip, and the pass was not valid there.

It was Memorial Day weekend when Mom and Dad drove me to Clif and Lucille's the night before I was to depart. My flight was a non-stop charter from Chicago to Orly Airport, outside of Paris. The plane was filled with college kids and educators, most of whom were on a shoestring budget and pretty lean on travel experience. There was an air of excitement and anticipation during the flight—and more conversation than I have witnessed on any flight since. I quickly realized I was one of the few passengers traveling alone. I also learned I was far better prepared for the next twelve hours than those around me. I knew Orly Airport was quite a distance from Paris proper. I knew where to catch the bus and how much it would cost. I knew where the bus stopped. I had studied the Metro system. I had exchanged enough money to last me until I could exchange more at the banks in Paris. I knew where the cheap hotels were. As I shared this information I became pretty popular in my section of the airplane. I also was studying my now dog-eared copy of *Let's Go Europe*. I even ripped out a couple sections of the book concerning places where I knew I wouldn't be going and gave those sections away.

I had one primary objective on that flight: to find someone fluent in French, with whom to share some of the Paris experience. Right on cue, one Julie Brayton, a University of Iowa co-ed from DeKalb, Illinois with several years of French language background, introduced herself. She was flying solo in Paris for a few days before meeting up with a girlfriend who was working as an au pair in France. She thought it best to have male companionship for safety. I was willing to trade my Y chromosome for her five years of French. We agreed to a mutually beneficial relationship for a few days. No, not that kind of mutually beneficial relationship. I was headed to Poland in search of *that* kind of relationship.

Julie and I had picked up a companion during the bus ride into Paris. His name was Eric. At 11:00 AM sharp Julie, Eric, and I were standing on the northwest corner of Rue something and Rue something else looking for John. I checked my watch once and then looked up to hear, "Hey, Pratt, I'm here just like I said I would be."

After a congratulatory high five, introductions, and a group hug, we set out to find lodging for the next couple of days. Rooms for four were hard to come by, so we settled on two rooms of two. John and I would share a room and Eric and Julie would share one. We asked to look at rooms in several of the cheap hotels that dotted the Left Bank before choosing a second floor room in one of them. It was clean and cheap with an "early drab" motif. The bathroom was down the hall, but our room did have a bidet. Had I not read about the bidet in *Let's Go Europe*, I am confident John or I would have peed into it. Since John and I had no plans for sex, we used the bidet as a place to chill our wine bottles and wash our underwear during the week.

To this day I am still not certain which culture is confused. Is it the French, where virtually every hotel room has a bidet, but many have no shower? Or is it the American culture, where every hotel room will have a shower, but scant few will have a bidet? Does this mean the French place a premium on specific body part hygiene, while the Americans settle for a more general approach to cleanliness? Or does one culture simply engage in more sex? I guessed this is what my teachers meant when they said we should all travel as much as possible to expand our horizons.

The next few days were filled with the obligatory tourist things. We went to the Eiffel Tower, Sacre Coeur, and Montmartre. The Arc d'Triumph, Champs-Elysees, Tuileriers, the Louvre, and Notre Dame took up a second day. Eric, John, and I took a train to Versailles and wandered the palace grounds for yet another day. It is an impressive place for sure. I was beginning to regret I hadn't paid closer attention in my European history classes.

We got lost in the town of Versailles and I stopped the first American we saw to ask directions. I knew he was one of us because he was wearing tennis shoes. Back then, tennis shoes were a dead giveaway. After receiving directions I continued the conversation.

"Thanks. So, where are you from back home?" I asked.
"Iowa," came the reply.
"Really? Me, too. Which town?"
"I'm from Clinton. It's over on the river."
"Yeah, I know where Clinton is. Do you know a guy by the name of Dick Eversoll? He's from Clinton and went to UNI with me."
The guy started laughing and said, "Dick Eversoll is a good friend of mine, and I went to UNI, too. I lived on tenth floor in Bender Hall. Where did you live?"
John and I both said, "No way! We were on eleventh floor of Bender Hall!"

We had lived one floor above this guy for two years and neither one of us knew him. But there we stood in the middle of Versailles, France, swapping stories about how cold Cedar Falls, Iowa gets in the winter. Go figure.

Ewa and I had agreed I would travel to Poland from Paris. The idea was that I would meet her family, see more of Poland, and maybe she could get the visas necessary to travel with me to other countries in Europe for a part of the summer. Timely communication on these points was more difficult to come by than you might imagine. Letters took about ten days to arrive. We didn't have home computers or the internet. Telephone calls had to be arranged twenty-four hours in advance. The fastest mode of communication was telegram. I had researched the Paris train schedules before I left the US and determined there was a train leaving about 9:00 AM from Gare du Nord (North Train Station) arriving around 4:00 AM the next morning in Poznań. The train would travel north out of Paris, briefly through Belgium, and then turn east through West Germany. It would continue on through East Germany and then to Poland. The train's final destination was to be Moscow.

The day before my departure from Paris I went to the station to purchase the ticket and to rehearse. Yes, you read correctly, *to rehearse.* This was going to be my first-ever train ride. I didn't understand how to get from one platform to the next. I needed to watch the departure and arrival boards to make certain I could read them. I wanted to listen to the arrival and departures as they were announced in French over the loud speaker. I hung out for a while watching people get on and off the train just to see if there was anything special they did that I might need to do, so as not to appear the novice I was. I then sent a telegram to Ewa telling her I had purchased the ticket and would be in Poznań in two days. Then John and I dined on *une baguette, fromage,* and *vin rouge,* because that is what you are supposed to do in Paris.

The next morning John and I said our good-byes and headed our separate ways. I have not seen or talked to John LaFalce since that day, June 4th, 1977. I hope he is doing well.

The train was originating in Paris, so I had ample time to board in advance of its departure. As near as I could tell there was no specific seat assignment but rather a class of ticket. I boarded the train a full thirty minutes before scheduled departure. I took the first cabin I saw, (it had room for six persons) and slung my backpack to the top rack and waited. I was soon joined by two older ladies who asked if the other seats were taken. Of course, I assumed that was what they were asking. For all the French I knew they might have been accusing the US of stealing the Louisiana Purchase. I smiled politely and nodded, gesturing that the seats were available. Rounding out our cabin were three young boys about eleven or twelve years old. I deduced they were German and were returning home from some sort of scout camp in France. They were speaking German among themselves but switching to French when some adults standing on the platform came to our window to say their final good-byes. I felt altogether inadequate at that moment. Here were kids half my age, traveling by themselves between countries, on a train, effortlessly switching between languages, who clearly felt none of the discomfort or apprehension I was feeling.

Here is where I can shorten the learning curve for any of you planning to take an extended cross continent train ride. Take some reading material and take some food. Of course, this is obvious to me now, as I am a veteran of such experiences. In June of 1977, I had *Let's Go Europe*, which by this time I had all but memorized, and seven Life Savers to occupy twenty hours. About an hour into our trip the old ladies opened their bags and out came bread, meat, cheese, and cake. I declined their first offer to share, but not their second one. Even the little boys took out some big chocolate bars and passed them around. All I had were two pineapple-flavored Life Savers. The only reason I had those remaining was because I don't like pineapple. I was too embarrassed to even offer to share.

We were in the middle of this communal dining session when the conductor came by to ask for our tickets. When he looked at mine, he punched a hole in it and repeated something to me several times in

French. I knew there was some problem but didn't know what it was. After a couple of tries he gave up and moved on to the next cabin. When he left there was quite a discussion among the other members of my compartment. They arrived at some settlement of the issue and we resumed our meal.

At our next stop in Aachen, a West German town on the border of Belgium, one of the young lads stood up to address me.

"Uhnt zer, I sink dees train ez no goot for you. Deez train, deez car, no goink to Polen. Deez car ez no goot for you."

Though heavily-accented this kid was clearly speaking his third language of the day and I understood, "Sir, this train is no good for you. This train and this car no going to Poland. This car is no good for you."

Holy cow! How could I have gotten on the wrong train, I thought. I had rehearsed. I did a dry run. I was certain I was on the right train. What did he mean? He took me by the hand and led me off the train to the platform. He then pointed to a sign on the side of the car. Each car had a sign on it bearing the name of a different city along our route. Finally, I figured it out. I was sitting in a coach whose ultimate destination was Hamburg, in the north of Germany. This car was being delinked from the train I was on. If I did not get into a different car, I was going to Hamburg. I needed to get my stuff and move to a different car. I ran back to retrieve my backpack and scoured the platform for a car labeled for Poznań. There was none, but I did find one labeled "Moskau." I figured any car headed for Moscow had to go through Poznań, so I got on. I was the only person in my cabin and one of only four or five in the entire car. I had a cabin all to myself for the next few hours. This gave me plenty of time to ponder the consequences had not that little kid taken me by the hand and mustered the courage to address me in his third language. I started to laugh. I was imagining how the telegram to Ewa would have read:

Dear Ewa, Stop
    Took wrong train. Stop. Am in Hamburg. Stop. Will get to
Poznań soonest. Stop. Sorry. Stop.
Tim

I was glad I didn't have to send that telegram.

I was really getting hungry, but I didn't know if this train had a dining car, and if it did, where it was located. I also had this irrational fear someone would steal my backpack if I left it. Looking back, I must have placed an extraordinarily high value on socks and underwear because that is about all any thief would have made off with, as I had the valuables around my neck in a secret pouch.

I finally broke down and nursed the final two Life Savers into submission. I still am not a fan of pineapple, but they were better than nothing.

At one of the early stops in West Germany, a red-haired woman I guessed to be about thirty poked her head into my cabin and indicated she wanted to join me. I motioned her in. Shortly after the train resumed we tried to communicate with each other. She was Polish and was also headed to Poznań. Now, I was starting to feel a little more comfortable. All I had to do was stick with this lady and I was certain to get to my end stop.

This was a great opportunity for me to practice Polish. Don't forget, I now had two full years of self-study under my belt. I told her I was from the state of Iowa in the US and was headed to Poznań to visit a girl. Surprisingly, she pulled out a Polish magazine and opened to an article about Triple X movie theaters and porn arcades in Waterloo, Iowa! I didn't know if I should feel honored this woman had heard of my state or embarrassed because of why she knew of it. In any event the remainder of the train ride was much more enjoyable.

As nightfall came we huddled close together for warmth. We shared a blanket as others joined our cabin. I was glad we got to our final destination when we did, because I was beginning to enjoy that ride more than I should. As it was, when we prepared to disembark in Poznań she gave me a hug and a little peck on the cheek. We exchanged winks as she embraced her husband and picked up her daughter.

It was 4:00 AM, give or take a couple of minutes, and I was hoping Ewa had received my telegram. She had. Within seconds of stepping off the train I spotted her. I was tired and hungry. I had not eaten anything since those pineapple Life Savers and that was two countries ago. But I remember an adrenaline surge when I saw her, or at least I thought it was adrenaline. Maybe it was some other hormone, I don't know. But I was very happy to see her. She told me the plan was to catch a 6:30 AM train bound for her hometown of Bydgoszcz. I wasn't too excited about two hours in the station followed by more time on a train, but I had a travel companion. I would keep this travel companion for the rest of the summer and the rest of my life.

It should come as no surprise the month of June had been planned out with a precision befitting a tour guide, only this time it was a tour group of one. We would stay three days in Bydgoszcz, travel to Szczecin for one week, and then go to Poznań for two days. After Poznań it was back to Bydgoszcz, then to Warsaw and on to Zakopane before returning to Bydgoszcz.

I was to stay with Ewa's sister and brother-in-law, Krystyna and Andrzej (Ahn–jay) Piasecki, while in Bydgoszcz, because there was no room at her parents' apartment. After a few hours of sleep, Ewa would take me to meet the family and have dinner at her parents' home. Knowing "one never gets a second chance to make a good first impression," I practiced my very limited Polish and quizzed Ewa on proper etiquette as we approached Sulkowskiego 54, apartment number 3, her childhood home.

There were handshakes, hugs, kisses, flowers, and many "*Witamy*"s ("Welcome"s) and "*Bardzo mi miło*"s ("It is my pleasure"s). Immediately I felt welcome. Aided by Ewa's translation, her parents first wanted me to tell my parents how appreciative they were of the hospitality my parents had shown their daughter during the previous summer. It was their turn to reciprocate. And reciprocate they did. Dinner was followed by a shot of vodka, coffee, and a birthday torte, in honor of my birthday two weeks earlier. Then Ewa's brother, Andrzej, brought out an accordion and accompanied everyone in the traditional Polish *Sto Lat* (One Hundred Years), which is sung for every festive occasion. All total there were nine of us that day at the Domagała home.

Domagała (Doh-mah-gow-uh) hardly sounded Polish to me. Every Pole I knew had a last name ending with "ski." But then again Des Moines, Iowa wasn't teeming with Poles like, say, Chicago. We are more the stomping grounds for the warm-blooded Scandinavians who can't bear the cold of Minnesota.

Sylwester (Dad), Maria (Mom), Andrzej (brother), Krystyna (sister), Andrzej (brother-in-law married to Krystyna), Zbyszek (nephew and son of Krystyna), and Małgosia (three year old niece and daughter of Ewa's other sister, Barbara, who was vacationing in Italy with her husband and son) were present to greet me that afternoon.

Fortunately, I was pretty familiar with the family tree long before I met any of them. It was a good thing, too. Follow this if you can. Ewa's oldest sister's given name is Sylweria (Sylvia), but she prefers to go by her middle name, Krystyna. Krystyna's husband is Andrzej (Andrew). Ewa's only brother is also Andrzej and is married to a woman named Krystyna. (She was not present that first day). So, at every family gathering and during every family gossip session it is necessary to identify which Andrzej you are speaking about, or speaking to. The same is required when addressing, or impugning, a Krystyna. When Ewa, her parents, and her sisters are talking of their brother, Andrzej, it is always prefaced by "nasz" ("our"). When talking of Andrzej the husband of their sister, they switch to just using his last name, Piasecki. This seems to work most of time. But this doesn't apply to the Krystynas. Among the parents and the siblings, Krystyna Piasecka (who was Krystyna Domagała before marrying) is referenced as Dzitka (an endearing carry over from childhood, meaning "little girl"). But the non-Domagałas feel less politically correct in using that name for their sister-in-law. And today's Krystyna Domagała, was yesteryear's Krystyna Stronska. One really needs a scorecard or telestrator to map the conversations. Maybe Ewa had met more of my relatives than I was going to meet of hers, but she wasn't caught in the middle of Abbott and Costello's "Who's on First" routine every time the family gathered.

After three days in Bydgoszcz, during which I played tennis with Andrzej on clay courts at the Zawisza Sports Club, attended the movie *Day of the Dolphins* (in English with Polish sub-titles), and lost numerous chess matches to Ewa's father, we caught the train for the northwest port city of Szczecin.

As I referenced earlier, Ewa's other sister, Barbara, and her husband, Jacek, were visiting Italy. They had taken their son, Piotr (Peter) with them and left their daughter, Małgosia (Margaret) in Bydgoszcz with Ewa's parents. Jacek was First Officer on a merchant ship. He helped to guide freight vessels all over the world. From time to time he would take his wife and family members with him. They lived in Szczecin and had told Ewa we could stay in their apartment if we went there.

You know how confident you feel the second or third time you do something, as compared to the first time? That's how I felt boarding the train for Szczecin. Heck, I had been halfway across Europe, through multiple countries. I knew how things worked. I spoke at least a little bit of the native language. My confidence was growing. Of course, all of this new confidence was unnecessary because I was traveling with the same woman who, less than a year earlier, had told the international press corps to sit down so she could see the next president of the United States.

We took a taxi. The address was Wilowa 10. We got in the little elevator and went up about four floors. There was a group of locks and Ewa had numerous keys. It was getting late. Ewa kept trying to turn the key in the lock. Something was wrong.

At first she passed it off as, "This stupid lock, they should get it fixed."

Then it was, *"Jasna Cholera,"* a mild Polish expletive.

Finally, it was total exasperation, "WHY WON'T THIS DAMN THING OPEN?!"

Then, as if Ali Baba himself had uttered the magic words, "Open Sesame," the door opened from the inside. There stood a man with the look of, "Why are you trying to break into my home?" on his face. My girl was on the wrong floor of the apartment building. For several minutes she had been working the door locks to the apartment belonging to Andrzej (yes, another Andrzej!) and Bogusia Gajda, not the one owned by Barbara and Jacek Różkowski. Just when I thought Mr. Gajda was about to reach for a club of some kind to defend his property, he said,

"Ewa? Pani Ewa? Bogusia, chodz tu, Ewa jest!" ("Bogusia, Come here. It's Ewa!")

To everyone's relief Andrzej and Bogusia recognized Ewa. The Gajdas were Barbara and Jacek's best friends and had met Ewa on a number of prior occasions. We shared a big laugh. Ewa introduced me and they invited us to come back to their place to play bridge after we settled in— at the correct apartment.

In Szczecin I began to get a real sense of daily life in Poland. People did not go to the supermarket once a week to buy a cart full of pre-packaged, highly-processed groceries. They went once a day to the little neighborhood shop to buy fresh eggs, rolls, bread, cheese, and meat. They would then stop by a *Ruch* stand (tiny little kiosks that could be found about every two blocks) to buy the newspaper and tram tickets. They might stop by the produce market to see which fruits were in season. One never had to walk more than three blocks for any of these items, which was a very good thing because he was going to stand in a line for all of them.

Ewa sent me out every morning to do the shopping. I wanted to "experience" life in Poland, and she was not going to deny me that opportunity. Late each evening she would give me a list of what I was to purchase the next morning. I would review the list and practice my Polish. *Ser, chleb, masło, mleko, kawa, pomidory* (cheese, bread, milk, coffee, tomatoes) were routine items, with some exotics, like *ciastko, piwo, papierosy* (cookies, beer, cigarettes) thrown in to expand my vocabulary. I stuck out like a sore thumb in the line at the neighborhood shop. I was immediately recognized as someone new. I could hear the whispers,

"Niemiec?" ("German?")
"Nie, ja myśle Amerykaniec." ("No, I think American.")

In these little neighborhood shops you were not permitted to just pull items off the shelf. You waited your turn in line and told the clerk what you wanted. The clerk would then fetch the items from behind the counter. This seemed terribly inefficient to me, but I guess if some of the inventory disappeared, the proprietor needed only to examine the employees and not the customers. I could sense the anticipation from the clerk and the customers as I approached the front of the line.

"Przepraszam, Panią, Ja nie mowię po Polsku bardzo dobrze, ale ja mowię po Polsku mało. Czy Pani, rozumie?" ("Excuse me, M'am, I don't speak Polish very well, but I do speak a little. Do you understand me?")

I had practiced these sentences so much I spoke them better than the swear words those Polish students had taught me back in Ames.

"Tak, słucham," ("Yes, I am listening") came the young female clerk's reply. The rest of the people in line were enjoying this little diversion in their morning.

I continued on, *"Masło, sześć bułek, i mleko, i ser, i chleb, i dwa jaja, po prosze."* ("Butter, six rolls, and milk, and cheese, and bread and two eggs, if you please.")

I got to the end of my order and everyone started to laugh, including the clerk.

If I wasn't self conscious before, I was then. Why were they all laughing at me? I paid the clerk and went back to the apartment. I made some coffee as Ewa got out of bed. She asked me how the shopping went. I told her I thought I had done really well, except at the end everyone was laughing at me, and I didn't know why. She asked me to repeat what I had said in the shop.

I rattled off the same list, *"Masło, mleko, ser, chleb,...i dwa jaja."* Then Ewa started laughing.
I said, "Yes, just like that. Everyone in the store did what you just did. Now, will you please explain to me why they were laughing."

Ewa went on to tell me that often times in Polish the slang form of the word "eggs" *(jaja)* is used as an alternative to "testicles," and I had just ordered two of them.

We went to a carnival-type celebration marking some anniversary of the local newspaper. We attended the Szczecin Philharmonic Orchestra performance, where Ewa tells me I fell asleep. We walked the banks of the Odra River along the main thoroughfare known as the *Wały Chrobrego*, but mainly I stood in lines.

One day I went to the "Pewex" store. This was a place where one could buy higher quality items and where there was a greater selection of goods. The one catch was that you had to pay in US dollars or some other "hard currency" from the West. When I got inside the shop I noticed that, unlike the neighborhood shop where I went for food every morning, this shop had two lines. I took my place at the rear of one of them and waited my turn. When I reached the front I told the clerk what I wanted. Here was a new twist. The clerk did not retrieve the item, instead she requested payment. She then gave me a receipt, and motioned me to the back of the second line, at the front of which I would be allowed to get my item.

At that moment I wondered if this was what Karl Marx had envisioned when he wrote his Manifesto. Then I began to wonder if the capitalist system, which I had experienced, was what Adam Smith had intended. One had a lot of time to ponder such things given the frequency with which one found himself in a line. This may be why average Poles seemed to be deeper thinkers than average Americans.

From Szczecin we traveled by train to Poznań. Ewa had just completed her master's thesis and was obliged to make an oral defense of this thesis before three professors at her university. This trip was just a quick overnighter to finalize those arrangements with her professors. Another of her college roommates and also an English major, Terry Mrozowska, was in Poznań working as an interpreter at the annual International Trade Fair. Terry had temporary housing in a separate dorm for the time she was working at the trade fair. We kept a low profile, so as not to put Terry at risk, when she agreed to secretly board us for the evening. We also confirmed arrangements to stay with Terry's parents in Warsaw a week later.

We headed back to Bydgoszcz. Ewa immediately returned to Poznań for the defense of her thesis. I was staying with Krystyna, Andrzej, and Zbyszek Piasecki, but each morning I was transported by Andrzej back to Ewa's parents, where I would remain with Mama and Małgosia. Sylwester (Ewa's father) was working part time as a bookkeeper at a meat production facility. Andrzej Domagała (brother) was working at his job in the Army. Andrzej Piasecki (brother-in-law) was working as a bus driver for the city of Bydgoszcz. Krystyna was working as a nurse. This left Mama, Małgosia, and me to while away the hours.

Mama was always cooking in preparation for the main meal. That meal was generally served around 2:00 PM – 3:00PM in the afternoon as everyone was arriving home from work. That's right, everyone was finished with their work days between 2:00 and 3:00 PM. They generally started their work days at 9:00 AM. Now I understood how they had time to stand in all of those lines. It was a "catch 22." They couldn't work too long or they wouldn't be able to stand in the lines. But if they were standing in a line they couldn't be working.

Here was my chance to repay the hospitality I was being shown. I volunteered (well, to be factually accurate, before leaving for Poznań, Ewa volunteered me) for two primary tasks: 1) to shop for whatever might be needed and 2) to entertain three-year old, Małgosia.

Sulkowskiego 54/3 looked out onto a very pretty park with lots of trees. There were permanent walking paths with benches and even a play area for small children. It was a great place to spend some time reading (though most of the material was in Polish) while Małgosia played. Each day Małgosia and I would also do some shopping. Invariably, Małgosia would do what most three-year olds will do—ask for candy, or gum, or ice cream.

"Wujek, kup mi lody." ("Uncle, buy me ice cream.")

This was not a directive but more of a timid request. Initially, I thought it was cute, and I bought her what she wanted.

As the week went on I began to gain some insight into the human condition as described by Freud. He says during early childhood we must all learn the merits of "delaying gratification" or we will fail to progress appropriately in our social development. Clearly, little Małgosia had me pegged for a sucker. Each day there were more requests for more items and I was feeling an obligation to "further her social development." I squatted down to her level so I could look her in the eye and told her,

"Dzisiaj, Wujek kupi lody, albo guma. Nie, lody i guma, tylko lody albo guma. Rozumiesz? Co, ty chcesz? (Today, Uncle will buy ice cream OR gum, not ice cream AND gum, only ice cream OR gum. Do you understand? What do you want?")

She nodded in total comprehension and chose gum. I felt pretty smug that I had done what thousands before me couldn't do—that is until ten minutes later when we passed an ice cream vendor and she threw a tantrum when I refused to buy ice cream. Then I just felt like a parent.

You may have noticed I was addressing Ewa's mother as Mama. Using the given name, Maria, would have been too informal, though I hardly think referring to a girlfriend's mother as "Mama" implies a higher degree of formality. The correct form of address to those deserving respect is *Pan* (for men) and *Pani* (for women). Perhaps I was subconsciously practicing for the future.

Mama was tall and slender. Her voice carried the effects of a lifetime of smoking. She was a woman in her early twenties at the time of the German occupation of WWII. She had been kicked in the head by some soldiers and periodically suffered headaches for the remainder of her life. Mama was a great cook, a skill she put on display while Ewa was in Poznań. I also learned Mama was even more curious about my relationship with her daughter than my own mother had been the previous summer. Though I spoke some Polish at the time, I found it very convenient to have only intermittent periods of comprehension. Here was a conversation Mama initiated no fewer than four times during Ewa's two day absence.

"*Dim!*" (Mama had misunderstood my name when I was first introduced to her. She understood "Dim" instead of "Tim" and that is how she addressed me for a long time. Some would argue her moniker for me was merely a commentary on my intellect, but again, I digress).

"*Dim, czy ty kochasz Ewe?*" (Tim, do you love Ewa?)

The question was just that direct and was accompanied by sign language which was impossible to misinterpret. This was not a question I was prepared to answer, especially to my girlfriend's mother.

"*Nie rozumiem,*" ("I don't understand") was my reply. She repeated her question and I repeated my answer. She waited a few hours and tried this again, but with no satisfaction from me. When Ewa returned from Poznań I told her what had happened and we laughed about it. But when Ewa thought I was out of earshot she admonished her mother for interfering in her personal life. I felt bad for Mama because, indeed, I was falling for her daughter.

Before leaving for Warsaw, where our primary task was to secure visas necessary for Ewa to travel with me for the rest of the summer, we had decided I would stay in Poland through July 12th. Ewa had been asked to be the godmother to Bartek, her brother's son, who had been born at the end of February. The baptism was scheduled for July 10th in the small town of Ujście, about one hundred kilometers west of Bydgoszcz. It was agreed we would return to Bydgoszcz in time for this event.

We caught a train to Warsaw where we stayed with Terry Mrozowska's parents in the suburb of Ursus. We got up early each morning to get to the various embassies as early as possible. There were prodigious lines at each embassy. We planned to visit Austria, Switzerland, West Germany and France. We quickly discovered the Swiss visa was easy to come by, so we focused our attention on the other countries. We first went to the Austrian Embassy where Ewa put me in the line behind thirty-five other people. Ewa went off to one of the other consulates to start the process there. We agreed she would return in two hours regardless of what she found at the other embassy. When Ewa returned she was shocked—and pretty angry, too—to discover I was further back in line than when she left!

I come from Iowa. Back home, when someone steps in front of you in line to inquire about something, generally it is because they have a good reason. I am not a "type A" personality and some would even describe me as laid back. Not wanting to appear the "ugly American," when a Pole moved in front of me in line I offered up little resistance, reasoning that I was on vacation and had more time than he or she did. His or her issue was probably more important than my own.

Ewa was incredulous.

"How can it be that you are further back in the line than when I left you?!" she ranted.

I mumbled something about how others appearing to have more pressing issues had "budged" (now there's a Midwest term for you) in line toward the front. No response was sufficient to quell her fury. It was obvious we would have to return the next day.
On the way back to Ursus, Ewa challenged me in much the same way I had occasionally challenged football teams at halftime.

"Man up! This is our house. Protect your own turf! Nobody, but nobody, takes what rightfully belongs to you! Take some pride in yourself! Remember all of the hard work that got you here! Focus on the mission and leave it all on the field!"

No, she didn't really use those phrases but the message was clear.

The next day, those other poor souls didn't stand a chance. I was fifth in line and we had the visa by 10:00 AM. The exhilaration continued through lunch at a cafeteria counter near the center of town. We were waiting in line (of course) to get a serving tray on which to put our food items. When Ewa and I got to the front of the line, there were only two trays left. She took one and, as I was about to take the last one, a little old lady stepped right in front of me and grabbed the tray. She might have gotten the tray from the Iowa Tim, but the new Polish Tim ripped it out of her hands and took his rightful place in line. Ewa was stunned at the monster she had created. I still feel bad about having done that.

West Germany denied Ewa a visa, but she was granted visas for Austria and France.

From Warsaw we traveled by train to Zakopane (Zah-ko-pahn-eh), a resort town in the Tatra Mountains near the Czechoslovak border. We decided to splurge a little and checked into the beautiful Kasprowy Hotel. I think this was the first time in my life I actually tipped a bellman to carry my luggage, and I tipped him very well. We were on a very limited budget knowing what money we had needed to last until my return flight from Paris on August 19th, but I didn't care about money right then. I had made a big decision.

There are some times in life when you don't want to ask a question until you are pretty certain you know how it will be answered. Asking someone to marry you is one of those times. Sales people are taught closing techniques to lead the customer to the buying decision. Books have been written teaching phrases like, "that makes sense, doesn't it?" or "there's really no reason not to do this, is there?" or "that would make things easier, wouldn't it?" which are intended to set up the final buying question. If there was a similar manual for marriage proposals, I hadn't read it. What I did know was this woman was pretty. She was smart. She was confident. She was assertive. She was fluent in three languages, and semi-fluent in two more. She was funny, and for some reason she actually seemed to like me.

As I took inventory of her numerous redeeming qualities, I felt it necessary to do some self examination to determine if there was any chance this girl would say "yes" if I asked her to marry me. I was smart. I was funny. I could sing a little. I could drive a bus, albeit too fast. I knew a lot about football and I knew she liked my family. I just wasn't convinced this would be enough to guarantee the answer I wanted to the question I was considering. Now I began to understand why guys do such sappy things when they propose. I am convinced it is because the groom's list of redeeming qualities is generally shorter than the potential bride's list. This means the guy has to do something to improve the odds of a favorable response. He has to impress with form over substance. He has to choose just the right time and place to pop the question. For me, that time was here and now in the mountains of Zakopane, Poland.

I wish I could tell you I made reservations at the restaurant and asked the waiter to place fresh flowers in a vase, and then to bring champagne. What really happened was we went to town, bought some bread and cheese, and made sandwiches. But I wasn't completely void of romance. When we returned to the hotel we took a walk into the forest which surrounded the hotel. After a requisite period of time walking hand in hand, we paused for a rest on a large log at the edge of the forest. I got down on one knee, (like I said, I hadn't read any manuals but I knew genuflecting increases the success rate in these moments), took her hand, looked into her eyes, and said,

"Ewa Joanna Domagała, will you marry me?"

She paused (for effect, I think) and replied, "Yes, Timothy Eugene Pratt, I will marry you."

We kissed. Since I had no ring to present to her we determined we must do something to memorialize the moment. I took out my pocket knife and for the next fifteen minutes, carved a heart into the side of a nearby tree. I put our initials inside and was even going to put the date, July 2, 1977. Then romance gave way to pragmatism. It was getting dark, the mosquitoes were biting, I was dulling the blade, and this carving thing was cramping my wrist. I would have soldiered on, but it was Ewa who said our initials were enough and we should head back to the hotel. Many years later we returned to the Kasprowy and searched for "our" tree. We couldn't find it because that section of the forest had been cleared to make way for a new ski run.

My visa was set to expire at 11:59 PM on July 4th. The two nearest towns where I could extend my visa were Kraków and Nowy Sącz. Kraków was a little closer, but since I had been there the previous year we decided to catch an early bus to Nowy Sącz on the 4th. The bus departed from Zakopane at 5:30 AM and arrived in Nowy Sacz before 9:00 AM.

We went straight to the government office where Ewa explained to the man at the information desk I needed to extend my visa. He informed her that this office only handled requests from foreigners for one hour— at the end of the day after the office closed. We were told to return at 2:00 PM. We had been the very first people in line and there were only a few people behind us. We even asked if we could wait until the locals were taken care of and then get my visa. No luck. We had to return at 2:00 PM. End of discussion.

The three and a half hour bus ride had me wishing we had gone to Kraków instead. There was nothing much to do in Nowy Sacz for five hours. We returned to the office around 1:15 PM so we could be first in line. To our surprise there was no line. Ewa inquired if we could go ahead and be processed a little early since there was no line. The lady told her we had better hurry because the office closed at two. Ewa said yes, she knew the office closed at two, but I was a foreigner and we were told I had to wait until after the office closed. Then the woman said we had been given wrong information. After two o'clock they remained open for one hour to process Poles. *During the day the office was open only to foreign nationals!*

In order to extend my visa, I was required to fill out a form, go to a bank to exchange ten dollars into złotys for each day I was requesting the visa extension, get a receipt, and return to the office. I had less than thirty minutes to complete all of this. We ran to the taxi stand. Five people were in front of us. Ewa was pleading in Polish to get us to the front. I had to cough up some money to leapfrog the five people. We ordered the taxi to take us to the nearest bank and for the driver to wait to take us directly back to the government office. This took about forty five minutes.

When we returned to the office it was closed, but there were people in the outer office.

Ewa went to work on the secretary. The Polish was flying fast and furious. My job was to look as helpless as possible while Ewa bullied, begged, cajoled, and pleaded to get us an audience with the guy behind the closed door. She succeeded, but when she explained my predicament to the gentleman he was unsympathetic. He said something to the effect that rules were rules. If he made exceptions for everyone his office would descend into chaos. She tried once, twice, three times and failed in each attempt to get the man to issue me a visa extension. Just when I thought all was lost, my Ewa began to cry. Right there in that man's office she stood next to him and sobbed. Between the crocodile tears she was explaining to the man that her boyfriend—no, her new fiancé—was required to leave the country by midnight. He would miss the christening of her nephew. He wouldn't be there when she told her family she was going to marry this guy from America. She skipped the part about how his incompetent staff had given us the wrong information and we had wasted an entire day in his town. Then she cried some more. He was trying to escort us out the door, but Ewa wasn't moving. Finally, he acquiesced, having determined the path of least resistance was to sign the document and stamp my passport extending my visa by seven days. That process took all of ninety seconds. We thanked him profusely and hastened to the exit. (Later, I determined the reason for his initial refusal was probably to elicit a bribe from us. I was just a little too naive to pick up on the signals. So much for the earlier comment about my skill at sensing non-verbal cues).

On our way out of the building I stopped at the information desk to address the man who had originally given us the wrong information. I looked straight at him and said, "You are a stupid son of a bitch!"

I knew how to say it in Polish, but chose to say it in English, fearing the consequences if he understood exactly what I was saying. Ewa immediately pulled me toward the door and said something about not pushing our luck. We returned by bus to Zakopane and prepared for a long travel day back to Bydgoszcz.

I had fallen ill with the flu on the train ride back to Bydgoszcz. With a steady diet of hot tea and chicken broth, Mama nursed me back to health over the following three days. This was just in time to make the journey to Ujście for Bartek's baptism.

The religious landscape in Poland has long been dominated by the Catholic Church. Today, approximately ninety percent of Poles identify themselves as Roman Catholics. In 1977, the numbers were similar but with a couple of obvious differences; there had not yet been a Polish Pope, and the Communist Party, which officially recognized no religion, was in power. Most Communist Party members were closet Catholics. It was once explained to me, several years later, this was kind of like being paid to play on one team but secretly betting on the opponent to win the game. This was the dilemma confronting Ewa's brother and many Poles at the time. Joining the Party improved your chances to further your career and provide for your family. It also meant you didn't flaunt your Catholicism, because Party members were not to believe in God. But even that was a charade, because there was a very strong possibility the Party boss above you was in the same boat. So, you can see there was a certain convenience in arranging young Bartek's baptism for the small town of Ujście, which also happened to be the home town of his mother. The chances Andrzej (Ewa's brother) would encounter one of his superiors, which might have created an awkward moment for both, at the church in Ujście were very remote.

Following the church ceremony there was a huge celebration. I counted about thirty people seated for dinner at the farm home of Andrzej's in-laws, the Stronskis. Little Małgosia's parents and brother had returned from Italy the previous day and were there. I was thinking this must have been the way Ewa had felt a year earlier when she was meeting all of my relatives. At my brother's wedding reception, Ewa had been the subject of a lot of conversations. On this day the tables were turned. I was the object of considerable interest at a gathering intended to honor a member of Ewa's family.

During dinner there were several toasts. There was a toast to Bartek, the featured attraction. There were toasts to the parents of the newly-christened baby. There were toasts to the grandparents and to the godparents. There was a toast to the visitor from America. With each tribute a little more alcohol was consumed, which was a good thing because I was in need of some liquid courage to make one more special toast. I gently rapped my spoon against my crystal wine glass to gain everyone's attention.

"Uwaga, uwaga. poproszę." ("Attention, please.")
I took the glass and after sneaking a peak at Ewa I announced,
"Za moją przyszłą żonę." ("To my future wife.")

There was a brief silence as everyone looked to each other, and to Ewa, to confirm what they thought they had heard. Ewa nodded in approval. Now there was even more reason to drink. I went over to Mama and gave her a hug and told her, *"Tak Mama, ja kocham Ewę."* ("Yes, Mama, I love Ewa.")

I confess all parties were a little unsteady as we boarded the train back to Bydgoszcz.

Chapter 6: Seasoned Travelers

The evening following the baptism we said our good-byes to Ewa's parents and headed for the train station. After securing Ewa's visas in Warsaw, we had made a very rough travel itinerary for the time after we would leave Poland. Since Ewa had no West German visa we had decided to make our first stop in Vienna, Austria. This required us to travel back to Kraków and through Czechoslovakia to get to Austria.

Poles needed no visas when traveling between the nations of Eastern Europe, but Americans did. When I had taken the train from Paris to Poznań a month earlier, I was required to have a "transit visa" just to enter East Germany on the train. The visa was good for twenty-four hours and basically allowed me to pass through the country. The visa was issued on the train and I had been charged about seven dollars for the privilege. I anticipated something similar for Czechoslovakia.

We took an overnight train from Kraków to Vienna. It was about midnight when our train crossed into Czechoslovakia from Poland. The passport control agents were accompanied by two soldiers with machine guns as they entered our car. The document inspection process was proceeding very quickly until they got to me. It was obvious that in 1977, not many Americans traveled the midnight train through Czechoslovakia. These guys took an inordinate amount of time reviewing my passport. They even got off the train with it, and went into their little hut and got on the phone. I know this because the little hut was right outside my window. I could see everything that was going on. Initially, I wasn't too concerned they had my passport. But five minutes became ten minutes, and ten became fifteen. They still hadn't returned my passport and the rest of the passengers were becoming a little agitated because we hadn't moved. Word had spread throughout our car there was an American on board and he was the cause of the delay.

One of the agents returned to our cabin and, in Polish, told me I owed eleven dollars—not złotys—only dollars, for the visa. I thought it was a little pricey but there wasn't much I could do. It was midnight on a Tuesday at the Polish-Czech border. It was not like I could call my ambassador in Prague and lodge a complaint. As luck would have it, I actually had twelve dollars in cash on me. All of my other money was in travelers checks and I don't think these guys would have cashed them for me. I was about to hand the guy the money and Ewa said, "Don't give him the money. A visa doesn't cost that much. He's just cheating you."

She even began a rather terse dialogue with the agent. I was telling her in English, as she argued with the guy in Polish, that yes, he was probably cheating me, but really it was OK. I just wanted to get my passport back and be on our way. Against Ewa's wishes I gave the man the money and he returned my passport, complete with the visa. My Ewa does not like to be played the fool.

We consulted the "the Bible" (as we now referred to *Let's Go Europe*) for instructions upon arrival in Vienna. We found a cheap hotel toward the western edge of the city. While in Vienna we visited Stephansdom (St. Stephen's Cathedral), the most recognized church in all of Austria, and the Spanish riding school where the famous Lipizzaner Stallions are trained. We never actually saw the horses because there was a fee to see the training session, as I recall. We were on a budget of twenty dollars per day and this was just the beginning of our journey.

My recollections of Vienna are pretty sketchy, but I do remember hearing waltz music everywhere we went. I could never figure out where it was coming from, but it was omnipresent. I think the department of tourism must have been piping it in.

While in Vienna we had decided our primary mode of transportation for the remainder of the summer was to be "*autostop*," or "hitchhiking," as I knew the term. My only previous experience with hitchhiking was when Darwin Yates, our next door neighbor as I was growing up, saw me walking home from Little League Baseball practice one night and pulled over to pick me up—and I didn't think that counted because I knew him, and I wasn't even hitchhiking when he did it. This was certainly one way to experience the continent and to stretch the budget.

We took the *U-bahn* to the last stop at the edge of town and located the main thoroughfare headed west. We stood side-by-side and stuck out our thumbs. I had no idea what to expect. Would we wait fifteen minutes or three hours?

After about an hour a trucker stopped. He was headed west and so were we. Our target, for no particular reason, was the city of Linz. I knew this was the boyhood home of Adolf Hitler, but more to the point, it appeared to be just about the right distance for a day's travel.

The trucker spoke no English. For some that might have been a problem. Not for me. I was traveling with my own UN language bank. Ewa will tell you her German is not all that good, but fluency is a relative term. After a two minute conversation with our driver she told me he was from the town of Steyr and would be going all the way to Linz. Like I said, fluency is relative. Though I was a little concerned as I watched our host drink two half liter bottles of beer, we were making good time. It was early afternoon and our trucker dropped us off at the outskirts of Linz.

Next, we were picked up by Wolfgang, a young businessman type. Wolfgang said we would much prefer Gmunden, about sixty kilometers to the south, over Linz. He told us Gmunden was a favorite vacation spot for locals. That was good enough for us. This was the kind of input we had hoped for when we had decided to hitchhike. He dropped us off in the middle of town where we found lodging in a small hotel. The next day we transferred to a room in a private home at half the rate.

Wolfgang, wherever you are, we owe you one. Gmunden is a picturesque town of about fifteen thousand people which sits on a lake and is surrounded by mountains. It is picture post card perfect. The weather was glorious. There was a castle, *Schloss Ort*, which appeared to float on the lake and was connected to the shore by a long pier. Every home looked as if it had been newly painted. Flower boxes, complete with flowers no less, adorned each residence. There was not so much as a single cigarette butt to be found on the sidewalks or in the streets. This town was a fairy tale.

Each morning we would sit on our balcony, look down at the lake, and enjoy the just-baked croissants with strawberry marmalade, which were delivered to our room. The pastries were accompanied by a small pot of coffee which would have made the most elite of Starbucks snobs green with envy. As we had only one deadline (to be in Paris on August 19th), we decided to extend our stay in Gmunden to five days. We wandered in and out of shops. We bought the *Herald Tribune*, so I could find out how the Yankees were doing. We read about some new hit movie, *Star Wars,* and we began a daily habit of working the Tribune's crossword puzzle.

While in Gmunden, I wrote a post card to my parents. It was the only one I sent for the entire summer. (I retrieved it from my parents' mailbox when it arrived a full week after I had returned from Europe. First class postage is not a priority on a limited travel budget).

I had never heard of Gmunden before Wolfgang had enlightened us, but I did know of our next destination—Salzburg. I probably should have known it was the birthplace of Wolfgang Amadeus Mozart, but must confess my interest in the city was because I knew *The Sound of Music* had been filmed there. Of course, when Ewa asked if I knew this was Mozart's birthplace, my reply was some sarcastic retort, delivered with just enough indignation to fool her into thinking I might have actually been aware of that bit of trivia—which, of course, I wasn't.

Outside of Gmunden we were picked up by three people in a station wagon. I thought there was no way we were going to get our backpacks and the two of us into a car which already appeared to be completely full.

But I also wasn't about to turn down a ride. Somehow it worked out and a few hours later we were in Salzburg waiting with thirty other backpackers to check into the youth hostel.

Youth hostels generally will open in the mid to late afternoon and accept tenants on a first-come first-served basis, provided one has purchased the Youth Hostel Association card. In the more popular European destinations lodging can be difficult to come by. Invariably lines would begin to form one to two hours before the hostel opened. We always found the people in the lines to be very civil, but I was grateful for my formal training in this regard, from the time spent in Poland.

Just ahead of us in line were five guys from New York City traveling in a roving pack of debauchery across Europe. You know how you sometimes say or do something as a part of a group that you would never say or do as an individual? That was these guys. No effort was required to eavesdrop on their conversation. I learned they were from New York, were in desperate search of females with loose moral convictions, and prided themselves on their capacity for alcohol consumption. I also observed that the big guy with the walking stick, and the kerchief around his neck, was perilously close to pneumonia. I pulled him aside and offered up about five blue and yellow capsules from the box of twenty to thirty my mother had given me before I left Chicago.

Here I need to explain that Mom was the head nurse at the free VD Clinic in Des Moines. Today, I think the correct term is STD (Sexually Transmitted Disease) Clinic, but in 1977, it was the VD (Venereal Disease) Clinic. Mom had access to antibiotics which would combat the spread of certain social diseases. When she presented me with my own personal box of these pills, she told me they were good for the treatment of many different infections, not just the sexually transmitted ones. I was to use them only in an emergency and only if I was certain I had an infection. Then, I should take them for ten days.

I shared this information (less the ten day part) with "Hoss" (because he reminded me of Ben Cartwright's middle boy) and made no promises the pills would work. He thanked me and then introduced the rest of the gang. They were far less obnoxious—almost pleasant—as individuals than they had been as a group. Even so, I really didn't want my girlfriend hanging with these panting dogs for the next two days, so I struck up a conversation with Tom and Becky.

Tom and Becky were from *Bahston* (Boston), had also arrived by *cah* (car), and were looking for another couple to go to the *bah* (bar) with them. After checking in, we obliged them and made plans to tour the city together the following day.

My photo album of that summer has a few snapshots with the caption, *Hohenzollern Castle, Salzburg, Austria*. In fact, the subject of those photos is Hohen*salzburg* Castle, which rises high above Salzburg, and is approximately 150 miles south and east of Hohen*zollern* Castle. (When you hang on the fringes of the tour group because you didn't pay for the English tour guide, truth and accuracy often become casualties).

We went to a park and dined on mettwurst, bread, and wine. I like different sausages, and I understand most of them are very distant cousins to the cows and pigs which form their base, but I prefer meats which are cut, not spread. Meat should not be squeezed from a tube. Sure, an occasional pate with a cracker at a social event is OK. Even a ham salad or a chicken salad is fine, but generally I want my protein to have a firmer texture. The mettwurst had the consistency of lard— probably because lard was its primary ingredient. We bought it because it was cheap and Ewa told me I would like it. She was wrong.

We stood outside Mozart's boyhood home. We walked the Mirabell Gardens. The adjacent Mirabell Palace is featured in one of the musical numbers of *The Sound of Music*, and entrance to the palace would have been included with the Sound of Music tour, had we chosen to allocate our limited resources for that purpose. Instead, we opted to quaff a few *biers* with our new best friends from the Northeast before returning to the hostel.

A much-improved Hoss and his posse were there to greet us when we arrived. Mom's blue and yellow capsules had cured whatever ailed Hoss. He told me he would "never ever make fun of people from Iowa again." I thought some more tangible token of appreciation would have been appropriate, but at least he said Iowa and not Idaho.

Salzburg is near the border with Germany and, since Ewa did not have a German visa, we were forced to retrace a portion of the route we had taken into Salzburg to get to our next stop, Zell am See. I have no recollection of the transportation to Zell am See, but I can briefly describe the town to you: it's a small town on a lake surrounded by mountains, pristinely clean, where every home appeared to be freshly painted, with a flower box hanging from every balcony. Sound familiar? I was beginning to think every hamlet in Austria could be described in exactly the same way. I wondered if all small towns in Iowa looked the same to foreign tourists. I determined they probably did. Waiting for rides along the highway offers up the same opportunities for deep contemplation as does standing in lines.

In contrast to Gmunden, this town appeared to cater to the skiing industry. The vertical rise above the town was more dramatic than Gmunden's and numerous ski runs converged at the town's periphery. We opted for just one night in Zell am See, reasoning if we stayed five nights at every beautiful quaint Austrian town we would never leave the country.

Tim and Ewa with Boston friends, Tom and Becky, in Salzburg, Austria

Choosing our route out of town was pretty easy. Walking to the west meant we would have to scale a portion of the Alps to get to the next town. Three hundred meters to the east would put us in the lake, and we had arrived from the south. By default, we headed north to the edge of town and waited... and waited... and waited some more. Finally, a young German fellow driving some sort of souped-up Alfa Romeo sports car, with a tiny back seat, took pity on us.

With apologies to Forrest Gump, I have to tell you, hitchhiking is "like a box of chocolates. You never know what you're gonna get." Ewa and her backpack crammed into the rear seat and I took my place riding shotgun. This was a tactical error. Our young driver was smoking Camel non-filters and listening to Pink Floyd's instrumental piece, *On the Run*, at a decibel level that made conversation nearly impossible. (Throw in a strobe light and substitute the Camel with a different kind of cigarette and you had Bruce Fisher's dorm room at UNI). He quickly determined the cute girl in the back seat was the one speaking German. When I am driving a car and want to carry on a conversation with someone in the back seat, I will sneak a peek in the rear view mirror to maintain eye contact with the person. You probably do the same. Not true of our young German chauffeur. He was compelled to turn and face Ewa as he spoke because he couldn't be heard above his own music!

Stay with me here. I was in the Alps mountains, on the passenger side of an Alfa Romeo sports car, with a chain-smoking Pink Floyd devotee, who was negotiating hairpin turns, at very high altitudes, while constantly turning his head to shout in German to my girlfriend in the back seat. With each passing kilometer I became more certain cancer was taking root in my lungs, but also realized it wouldn't matter because I wasn't going to survive this ride, anyway.

Mercifully, there was a break in the music. He then turned to me and pointed toward the stopwatch that was somehow attached to his steering wheel! The only words I understood were "Niki Lauda" (the great Austrian Formula One driver who had been in a fiery crash the previous year). He then clicked on the stopwatch and my head snapped back as the car found another gear. We were now in a valley with a line of about eight cars ahead of us. As the tape kicked over to the next Pink Floyd track he crossed the center line and passed all eight cars before returning to our lane. I glanced over at the speedometer and did some quick math in my head. One hundred seventy kilometers times point six two equals….good God! We were traveling over one hundred miles per hour! I braced myself against the dash, closed my eyes, and quietly repeated, "He doesn't want to die any more than you do. He doesn't want to die any more than you do." I think we had been in the car for less than thirty minutes when he pulled over and announced he was going right, and we needed to go left if we were to get to Innsbruck. It was a good ten minutes before the color returned to my knuckles.

A series of two or three short rides got us to the edge of another small town, St. Johann in Tyrol. It was the middle of a Saturday afternoon and there was a dearth of traffic. We were beginning to think this was where we would have to spend the night. We were learning the hard way that hitchhiking was best done during the week. More families and couples traveled on weekends with less room to take on added passengers. We feared one night in St. Johann in Tyrol would become two nights, and we still had a lot of Europe to see.

We had been waiting about two hours when Ewa offered up an idea. She told me to cross the street and try to blend in with the building about fifty meters up the road. She would try to catch us a ride as a solo. We knew it was underhanded, but we were getting desperate. I had barely crossed the street when I turned around to see not one, but two cars stopping to offer Ewa a ride. I maintained a low profile as Ewa told the young single driver of the first car she was bound for Innsbruck. What a coincidence, so was he. He opened the door and motioned her in. It was then Ewa called to me and said she had secured a ride. I ran back to the car, retrieved my backpack from the ditch (where we had stored it just out of the view of oncoming traffic), and followed Ewa into the car. I could read the whole cycle of emotions on the poor guy's face. In a span of ten seconds he went from absolute excitement, to shock, to anger, and finally to resignation. He had been scammed. He was probably thinking that a good-looking single girl hitchhiking in the middle of nowhere on a Saturday afternoon was probably too good to be true. And he was right. We had very little conversation, but he did smile as we thanked him when he let us out in Innsbruck.

The 1976 Winter Olympics were held in Innsbruck. You might remember this is when Franz Klammer, the Austrian downhill skier, captured the gold medal on the home turf with a riveting, daredevil, sixty mile per hour descent down a mountain known as Patscherkofel. He was the final skier of the medal contenders and the weight of the entire Austrian nation was on his shoulders. He trailed at the halfway mark, went airborne, and even skied a brief moment on one ski on the lower part of the course. It was probably the most dramatic race in the history of that sport.

I wanted to trace Klammer's path down that mountain, but the closest I got was a picture taken from near the youth hostel where we stayed. I later found out I had the wrong mountain in the photo, but I figured one mountain looks like the next one.

The most impressive Olympic sights were the two ski jumping ramps. I understand the 1976 Olympic Ski Jump Tower was demolished and replaced with a new one in 2002. The 1976 Tower rose about one hundred fifty feet above the ground. I have to believe ski jumpers are a "few bubbles off plumb." It looks to me as if their sport is akin to skydiving without a parachute. The view at the top is incredible though. I'll give them that.

We walked the streets of Innsbruck and stopped to watch several games of lawn chess in the Burrgarten. It was a lazy overcast Sunday afternoon and we really didn't do too much. We were anxious to move on to a new country.

We awoke to a bright sunshine suggesting it should be a little warmer than it was. By now we knew travel itineraries were arbitrary, at best, when *autostop* was the principal means of transport, but our sights were set on St. Moritz, Switzerland as the final stop for the day's journey.

A trucker picked us up almost as soon as we put down our backpacks. When he dropped us off, two young kids, about our age, followed soon after. We chalked up our good fortune to the fact this was a Monday. We were certain to make St. Moritz by the middle of the afternoon. Well, maybe not.

I am not a huge fan of TV game shows, but I do occasionally watch Jeopardy to see if I know the answers, or—pardon me—to see if I know the *questions* to the Jeopardy answers. Like the little boy who pretends he is batting with two outs in the bottom of the ninth, the bases loaded, and his team trailing by three runs, I sometimes imagine I have wagered all of my money on the Final Jeopardy category of *European Potpourri*. Alex Trebek then says, "And the Final Jeopardy answer is… the four national languages of Switzerland."

I watch as my opponents each rattle off Italian, French, and German, but none correctly identifies the fourth. The drama builds because I can only be the Jeopardy Champion if I have wagered everything and can name all four languages. Alex pushes the button to reveal my answer:

"What are German, French, Italian, and… *Romansh?*"
"That's absolutely correct and Tim, you are our new Jeopardy Champion!"

How do I know this answer you ask? Well, I have shared a Volkswagen Beetle with two of the sixty-five thousand people on this planet who speak that language. They were an older couple who picked us up about twenty miles before the Swiss border and dropped us off less than a mile after we entered Switzerland. It wasn't all that odd that *I* didn't recognize the lingo. But when my personal linguist struggled to communicate, I knew this wasn't one of the mainstream languages taught at most universities. Ewa tried once or twice to talk with them in German, but when I asked her what they said she replied, "I have absolutely no idea." I secretly thought to myself, "Now you know how I feel."

The weather had begun to rapidly deteriorate and there were very few cars headed in our direction. The sky turned overcast, the winds picked up, and the temperature dropped about thirty degrees. Then it started to rain. Panic was about to set in when a prosperous-looking middle-aged couple, in a big Mercedes, rescued us from the elements. They were headed to the town of Scuol.

Even though we had only traveled a total of seventy-five miles we decided to stay the night in Scuol. As we were walking to the nearest hotel, a woman on the street stopped us with the words, "*frei zimmer*" ("vacant room"). After a few minutes of intense negotiating Ewa told me we should follow this lady. We had just rented a room in her home for the evening; it even included breakfast, but a shower was extra. The decision to stay in Scuol had been a good one, because the next morning we awoke to see snow had fallen in the higher elevations. Had we continued to hitchhike,we would have been doing so in a snowstorm.

St. Moritz was only about an hour away. We were in town before noon courtesy of an Australian mate who bid us "g'day" as he deposited us in the center of town.

I had watched some famous bobsled competition on ABC's Wide World of Sports where the announcer had said St. Moritz was a playground for the *uber* wealthy. It reeked of money. We window-shopped at Gucci, Van Cleef and Arpel's, and Cartier (the only one of the three I had ever heard of), and wondered who had the money to shop at those places.

Tim practicing "Autostop" in Switzerland

St. Moritz was beautiful, to be sure, but it was almost too perfect: bright sunshine, a lake with Chicago Cub-blue water, and rugged snow-capped peaks. It reminded me of that rare girl in your high school who was so drop-dead gorgeous you never even thought about asking her out because you just knew she was out of your league. St. Moritz was Luann Wilkinson. We hiked some trails above the town, did our daily crossword and made plans to leave on Friday, so as not to hitchhike on the weekend.

We were eating breakfast in the hostel dining room when we heard two British girls having a discussion about which day of the week it was. In this regard, backpacking around the countryside is like being retired; you lose track of what day it is. I was pretty certain it was Thursday but the one girl insisted to her friend—and to me when I inquired—today was Friday. After some discussion Ewa and I decided it must be Friday and we should hit the road to avoid the perils of weekend hitchhiking.

We quickly packed and walked to the main road just as it began to rain. I gave Ewa the new poncho I had purchased before leaving Iowa. We waited and we walked. We waited some more and we walked some more. During one of the waiting times I told Ewa I was certain we had made a mistake. I was now positive today was Thursday and not Friday. This was not what she wanted to hear. An argument ensued. This was our first really big disagreement. It was cold; we were wet; and Ewa had convinced herself it was all my fault.

I was soon to learn how Ewa's anger would manifest itself. For the next two hours my every attempt at communication was met with total silence. I wanted to "discuss" the issue and resolve it. She did not respond. I admonished her for child-like behavior. I got silence in return. I tried to joke about how cold and wet we were. Nary a peep. She walked ten paces ahead of me. Just as I caught up with her, she took off again. We had been starting and stopping for three or four miles. In fact, we had walked all the way to the next town of Silvaplana with not one word exchanged between us. I had already figured out there would eventually come an end to this cold shoulder, but I was powerless to influence its timing. Finally, a guy about my father's age offered us a lift. He said he was going to Chur. Ewa decided we were going there also. The silence barrier was broken when the driver asked us to join him for a cup of coffee along the way. It would be his treat. We had to talk since he was buying the coffee and asking us questions about where we had been and where we were going. Make no mistake, if there had not been third party intervention I am confident my Ewa would have traveled the rest of Switzerland and all of France in total silence. Fortunately, the years have mellowed her in this regard.

My only recollections from the town of Chur are the uphill climb to the youth hostel and the absence of hot water in the bathroom. It is a shame I have been to such a beautiful place (I looked at some pictures on the internet because apparently neither Ewa, nor I, took any photos) and only remember a cold shower. Has that ever happened to you? Not the cold shower part, but when you've gone to some place new and your only memory is of something annoying? My high school Spanish class traveled by bus, for ten days, to various cities in Mexico one summer. Against advice to the contrary, I drank water straight from the tap. All I remember of Mexico City is the bathroom of the hotel room I shared with Chip Elefson and Lowell Long. I suspect some of you have had similar experiences.

The first ride of the following day was from a young fellow who was himself a seasoned hitchhiker. He worked for 3M, spoke fluent English, and took us grocery shopping. And when he dropped us off at the edge of St. Gallen, he printed a sign indicating our next destination: Zurich.

The Zurich hostel was run with the efficiency one would expect from the German Swiss. It was immaculate. When we checked in, each person was given a set of sheets and a blanket along with a page of instructions. "Lights out" was at 11:00 PM. Everyone had to leave for the day by 10:00 AM. There were other rules but what caught my attention was the part that said any violators of the house rules would be removed from the facility without refund. I said it was efficient, not friendly.

The sexes were divided into different hallways with three to a room. Any odd lots (of which I was one) would be matched together in sequence. Well, the guy in front of me was some fellow named Lev, from Jerusalem. The kid behind me was a Muslim from Egypt. I was not particularly well-versed in Middle East politics, but I did know enough about the Six Day War of 1967, and the Yom Kippur War of 1973, that putting an Arab Muslim and a Jew in the same dorm room might require more than a Christian from Iowa to moderate the discussion. Much to my surprise, after we introduced ourselves they each made some comment about not wanting to discuss politics. The evening progressed without incident. Given the Middle East turmoil of the past thirty years, it appears as if neither of my roommates from that evening in Zurich has ascended to a position of influence his respective country.

Zurich had the look and feel of an important city but lacked the awe-inspiring panoramas of the mountain towns. We decided weekend hitchhiking would be easier between big cities and concluded we would rather spend more time in Lucerne than Zurich, so we stayed a single night in Zurich.

We needed just one ride from a Pakistani in an old beat up blue Fiat to get to Lucerne.

As we were searching for a hotel we bumped into Tom and Becky, our Boston friends from Salzburg. This was less of a coincidence than one might think. In fact, it was a fairly frequent occurrence that we would meet people on the street in one city who we had seen at a youth hostel in a different town. I guess this just makes sense. We were all seeking cheap lodging and transportation and in search of the same tourist attractions. Tom and Becky had arrived by train and had acquired new best friends with whom to share Lucerne. That was fine with us, as Ewa was not feeling well and she spent most of the next two days in bed.

I scouted the area to get the general layout and to locate the essential facilities: a market, a bank, a bar, and the bus stop. I even found a small movie theatre nearby. We had been very loyal to our daily budget and planned to splurge with a trip to the top of Mt. Pilatus via the cogwheel railway. Others had told us the view of Lucerne and the surrounding area from the summit was breath-taking. Since Ewa was not feeling well, and it had been pretty cloudy, we opted against spending the money.

We also observed a lot of free entertainment on the streets. The Swiss flag was everywhere. There was a celebration atmosphere throughout the town. I heard a woman speaking English at a flower stand and inquired as to the cause for the festive occasion. She replied that it was Swiss Independence Day.

"Independence from whom?" seemed to be a natural follow up. She had no clue, but then confessed she was a tourist from Sweden.

I'll save you the trouble of researching the answer on your own. Swiss Independence Day is August 1st and dates back to a reference made to "early August" in the Federal Charter of 1291 (you remember that one don't you?), when the Swiss apparently declared their sovereignty from the Holy Roman Empire! There was some confusion as to the date because in 1993, the Swiss held a national vote on whether they should celebrate independence on August 1st or November 8th. It is my opinion that if a country's citizens have to vote as to which day they should celebrate their independence, then the motive is not recognition of their autonomy. Rather, they may have a complex because every other nation gets to acknowledge its birth, and they feel left out. I guess this is a natural consequence of seven hundred years of peace.

We walked the six hundred plus feet of Kapellbrucke (Chapel Bridge), which our guide book told us was the most photographed structure in Switzerland. Kapellbrucke is a covered bridge spanning a river that drains Lake Lucerne. (It was badly damaged by fire in 1993, but has since been rebuilt). There were paintings dating to the 1600s on the inside of the bridge and a brick water tower at one end. It was good for Ewa to get outside, but when it started to sprinkle we were glad we were on—or is it "in?"—a covered bridge. We finished the evening at the movies where we watched Walter Matthau and Tatum O'Neal in the *Bad News Bears*. Ewa consented only because it was near the hotel and was in English.

Interlaken, Switzerland rests in an Alpine valley at an elevation some two hundred feet higher than the highest point in all of Iowa—a mound in a hog lot on a farm in the far northwest part of the state. (The spot was dubbed "Hawkeye Point" several years ago and rises all of 1,670 feet above sea level). Interlaken serves as the jumping off point for a number of summer and winter activities in the rugged Bernese Oberland section of Switzerland. We had no trouble finding one of the several hostels after being deposited near the east train station, courtesy of our latest Good Samaritan—a fellow with bright red hair who was trying to convert the entire world to Christianity, one soul at a time. I think he was almost disappointed when I told him I had six uncles or cousins, on my mother's side, who were Lutheran ministers. Saving souls was kind of like the family business.

After some grocery shopping (we again purchased mettwurst, this time by mistake) we dined in the commons area of our hostel. It was there we met Bob and his friend, Lori. They were from Minneapolis. Their plan was to hike the Kleine Scheidegg the following day and they asked if we would like to join them. Kleine Scheidegg is a mountain pass between a couple of very impressive peaks, the Eiger and Lauberhorn. I was game for the adventure though a little more reticent than was Ewa. We had done some hiking around St. Moritz, but from Bob and Lori's description this Kleine Scheidegg was going to be a step up in class and might require a greater degree of fitness than our previous efforts. Lori was in training for a marathon. Bob was a slender fellow who appeared to be in pretty good shape. I got the impression these two had done this sort of thing before.

Bob and Lori drove us to Grindelwald. There were multiple entry points to the main path leading to Kleine Scheidegg. They merged into one primary path at the higher elevations. At the lower levels the path was paved asphalt, so it was very easy to identify against the backdrop of the rising peaks. I quickly determined that Lori's pace of ascent was far different from what I had planned. We were less than two hundred meters into our climb, and Lori was already a full fifty meters ahead of the three of us. I don't think she turned around once in the first twenty minutes. Then she stopped for a sip of water. We hustled to catch up to her. I surveyed the panorama as I took a few...okay, several...breaths. I looked down on where we had been and then looked up to where we were going. As I was assessing my resolve to continue, Lori bolted forward at a power walker's pace, and the others followed. "What's the hurry?" I thought. Was she meeting someone at the top? Was there a finish line with a tape at the summit? Had she heard that rain might be expected, even though there was nary a cloud in the sky? Or, had she been inspired by Billie Jean King's thrashing of Bobby Riggs in the Battle of the Sexes Tennis Match in 1973? Whatever her motivation, for the next several hours our foursome was the equivalent of those autobahn drivers who ride your rear bumper, while flashing their headlights and left-turn blinkers. We were the "passers," not the "passees."

During the climb we did stop long enough to drink water directly from a mountain stream. Some goat farmer had braced a long, hollowed-out, wooden plank square in the middle of some trickling water on the hillside. The plank extended from the water at a forty-five degree angle diverting it to a nearby trough. As we drank from the trough, the free-roaming goats literally ate the sweater which was tied around Ewa's waist.

At the summit of the pass, Lori permitted us some time to recover. We dined on bread, cheese, and soda which I had carried from the bottom. Bob was doing fine. Ewa showed no ill effects from her pack-a-day cigarette habit, but my legs were like jelly. I was fearful Lori was going to suggest we should scale one of the mountains in front of us.

The Eiger, Monch, and Jungfrau are the three primary peaks staring you in the face at the pass summit. It is as if you can reach out and touch them. The Jungfrau stopped growing at 13,642 feet. The view was spectacular. There were a lot of people atop Kleine Scheidegg, but most had arrived on the Jungfraubahn, a cogwheel train which travels daily from Grindelwald and continues further to the highest rail station in Europe. During our hike we had climbed well over three thousand feet in elevation. It was time to head down.

The roles were reversed on the descent. Try as they might none of the three could keep up with me. At first Ewa thought I had been overcome with some raging bout of machismo and was trying to prove I was as fit as the three of them. Then she realized my rapid pace was less about ego and pride and more about physics. Isaac Newton taught us, "an object in motion will stay in motion until acted upon by some outside force." A low center of gravity, additional body mass, and fatigued legs combined to make stopping nearly impossible at places where the pitch was steep. At times I had to run to catch up with my own body lean to keep from rolling down the mountain. I kept looking for one of those ramps like they have in Colorado for runaway trucks. I think a few people were spun completely around as they were sucked into my wake. Fortunately, there were intermittent occasions of flat terrain allowing me to safely negotiate the way down. I was exhausted, soaked in sweat, and ready for a beer.

Back at the hostel we showered, ate, rested, played some cards and met Charlie. Charlie was an interesting, well-read, thoughtful, free-spirit sort of chap from Virginia. He was planning an excursion to the top of Schilthorn for the following day. At Schilthorn's summit is a revolving restaurant, Piz Gloria. The mountain and the restaurant were featured prominently in the 1969 James Bond film, *On Her Majesty's Secret Service*. This was an all day event from Interlaken where one would take a bus, a train, a funicular, and a cable car to reach Piz Gloria. It was going to be expensive, but this was our reward for not taking the cogwheel train to Mt. Pilatus back in Lucerne. It was also a chance to recover some electrolytes that had been lost during the previous day's climb.

The view from the top of Schilthorn is magnificent—at least that's what others have told me. The post cards sure are pretty. I know. I bought one so I could show everyone back in Iowa what I would have seen, but for the fog. Look out your nearest window right now. Imagine if you took the white cotton sheet from your bed and covered that window. You would still be able to see more of what is on the other side of the window than we could see from Piz Gloria. The thought crossed my mind this might even be an elaborate Disneyland-like ride. From the time we boarded the final cable car at a place named Gimmelwald until we reached the summit, we could see only the others in our gondola. We had no idea if we were suspended two feet or two thousand feet above the valley floor. I wondered if anyone had ever seen the top of Schilthorn. Maybe this was some elaborate tourist trap and I was simply the most recent fool parted from his money. Maybe this was the Swiss equivalent of the Iowa farm boy daring the unsuspecting city slicker to urinate on the electric fence. Of course, as we descended to Gimmelwald and then to the next town of Murren, the fog began to burn off. (This is the lesser-known addendum to Murphy's Law which states, "…that which has gone wrong will be righted, once Tim Pratt has lost sufficient money." Back then it was true at Schilthorn. Today it applies to the stock market).

There is a paved trail which connects Murren to Lauterbrunnen, the next town further down the mountain. We decided to walk. My faith in all things Swiss was restored over the next several hours.

The Lauterbrunnen Valley is home to over seventy waterfalls. The walk from Murren to Lauterbrunnen to Stechelberg will affirm any beliefs in a higher power. The dramatic rise of the cliffs from the valley floor, the sounds of the cascading water, and the smell of the mountain fresh air coalesce in an orgy for the senses. To describe that afternoon stroll as beautiful, or breath-taking, or awe-inspiring, is to describe Secretariat as a fast horse—technically accurate, but woefully inadequate. We picnicked with Charlie and three others at Trummelbach Falls. The day was cool and still overcast but there was no question we were in one of the "must see" places on this planet. I enthusiastically recommend each of you to add a visit to the Lauterbrunnen Valley, Switzerland to your "Bucket List."

We were now just two weeks from the return flights to our respective home countries. We needed a little firmer agenda for the next ten days. We worked back from our scheduled departure date. At a minimum, Ewa wanted a full week in Paris. It was decided we would split the next seven days into two cities, Lausanne and Geneva. We would just pass through Bern, and bypass Basel altogether.

A young teacher on holiday was the first to offer us a ride. She was returning to her hometown of Bern, the capital city of Switzerland. We ducked into a small market to buy some bread and meat for lunch. I made certain we did not get mettwurst. Generally, we drank the cheapest soda, usually Fanta Orange or a generic cola, when we were hitchhiking. Wine was our preferred choice when we were stationary. After a quick lunch at a park in Bern we hit the highway. Three drivers and three hours later we were in Lausanne.

Lausanne rests on the northern coast of Lake Geneva (Lac Leman) in the French section of Switzerland. The city almost seems terraced as it rises from the shores of the lake. Our "bible" told us Lausanne was probably the most cosmopolitan of all Swiss cities. I guess this made me feel more sophisticated. I doubted any city in Iowa had ever been labeled as *cosmopolitan,* unless it was Des Moines, as described by someone from Algona. We walked everywhere in Lausanne. Our hotel balcony presented a great view of the Cathedral of Notre Dame, not to be confused with the Notre Dame Cathedral of Paris. We walked to Mon Repos Park, where we viewed an exotic birds exhibit. We strolled along the shores of the lake and enjoyed the beautiful clock of flowers in Ouchy. We spent hours working the daily crossword puzzle and just relaxing in the park areas along the lake front. I would have demanded a visit to the Olympic Museum had it existed in 1977.

I was the navigator in our group of two—and still am for that matter. Even today my children will tell you one of my favorite sayings is, "There are two things you have to know in life: where you are and where you're going." In this context, I am referencing life in general, though I often use the phrase in a more literal way as they inquire about how to get somewhere. Lausanne was an easy city in which to determine directions. It appears to tumble from the foothills to the lake front. Uphill was north and downhill, toward the lake, was south. That part was pretty simple. We descended to the lake via stairs tucked along the sides of homes and buildings, which allowed pedestrians access to different levels in the city. Think of a terraced effect and you have the general idea. The challenge was to remember which level we were on and the location of each set of connecting steps for our return from the lake. Ewa was not particularly good at this. On more than one occasion, I walked a few paces behind her as she searched in vain for the next set of stairs that would lead us in the direction of our hotel. When she eventually turned around, I poked a little good-natured fun at her routing deficiencies and charted the correct course. I was to get my comeuppance a week later in Paris.

Geneva shares Lac Leman with Lausanne. They are separated by less than fifty miles and both claim French as their language of choice. A young fellow in a laundry truck was kind enough to transport us from Lausanne to the center of Geneva.

My prior knowledge of Geneva was limited to being aware it was home to the League of Nations and the Jet d'Eau. Following *The Great War*—as WWI was known before we felt the need to begin numbering them—the League of Nations was established in an effort to reduce the likelihood of a future global conflict. Obviously, it failed. President Woodrow Wilson was one of the strongest League advocates, but he could never convince our Senate to ratify the Treaty of Versailles, which would have required our membership in the League of Nations. The Jet d'Eau is a waterspout on Lac Leman that shoots water over four hundred feet into the air. When we first saw the water shooting into the air we did not have our cameras with us. When we returned to the lake front the following day, the spout had been shut off, so we took several pictures of each other. I am almost ashamed to admit that post-Geneva, I knew little more of the city than I knew pre-arrival. We had been traveling for a solid month and one museum was beginning to look like another. One beautiful lake was also beginning to look like another, only in this case it was the same lake. Ewa was storing her culture-awareness and sight-seeing energy for one final push in Paris.

A University of Michigan grad student took us to the border town of Gex, just inside France. There we were picked up by a young French woman who knew a short cut. For the second time on our journey we crossed the 100 mph barrier and held on for dear life. We were near the town of Dole when she let us out. We resumed hitchhiking just in time to catch the startled look on the faces of a couple who had passed us by just before the young girl had given us a ride. It was as if they were in some cartoon. We recognized the car and the couple as they drove past us. We saw the double take as the wife gestured to her husband indicating something like, "How did they get here?" We just smiled.

Paris is more than two hundred miles from Geneva, and we had not traveled half that distance in any one day since Vienna. We hoped to make it as far as Dijon... until Delfino came along. Delfino was an Italian businessman headed to Paris. Though it meant a late arrival (7:00-8:00 PM), we decided to go straight to Paris and accepted the longest— and last—ride of the summer.

We had decided to look for lodging in the same area where I had stayed with John LaFalce two months earlier. I was a little disoriented when we emerged from the Metro station. As we were discussing which direction was best, Ewa heard a couple speaking Russian. She immediately went to them and asked them to point us to the Left Bank section of town. "Go up two blocks, turn left, go one block, and you will be near the Sorbonne. From there you will know what to do." Ewa translated from Russian to English for me and we did as instructed. After walking only one block Ewa stopped a German couple and asked if we were going the proper direction. This couple repeated the same instructions as had the Russians. Again, Ewa translated to English and parroted them back to me. With some degree of indignation, I responded, "You just asked directions at the last corner. I know what to do now. You don't need to stop every block to ask directions. Can't you remember what that couple just told..." Before I could finish the sentence, she started in, "Look here. I have to remember the words to all of these languages. You should at least be able to remember where we are!" I had no good reply. She was right, of course, just as she has been right so many times since that day. But she still is only so-so at directions.

When John LaFalce, Eric, and I had toured the sights of Paris, I think it was mostly about being able to say we were there. That's probably what travel is to a lot of folks, a sort of status symbol. Don't get me wrong, I think it is inevitable that one will learn from any travel experience, and I certainly believe in the benefits which accrue to all parties when people venture abroad. I just sometimes wonder what is behind the initial impetus to go. I don't wonder about Ewa's motivation. It is a genuine thirst for learning and self improvement. I know that sounds cliché, but it is so very true.

As you might expect, we toured all the sights of Paris I had visited earlier in the summer, including Versailles (where I realized John, Eric, and I had missed over half of the palace grounds during our visit). Ewa was just getting started. We went to Pere Lachaise Cemetery. This was a mandatory stop because most of Fryderyk Chopin is buried there. (His heart is in a pillar in a church in Warsaw, honoring his dying request to return his heart to Poland). While on the Ile de la Cite to take in Notre Dame, Ewa forced me to go a few extra blocks to Sainte-Chapelle, home of the finest rose windows of stained glass to be found anywhere in the world. It was not enough to re-trace the Louvre and to find the Mona Lisa. We had to go to Galerie Jeu de Paume. This was a much smaller museum at the edge of the Tuileries Gardens which, at that time, housed the works of impressionists Salvador Dali, Pablo Picasso, Vincent van Gogh, Claude Monet, and Edouard Manet. Sue Williams, my elementary art teacher who once gave me a "D" (and she was being charitable) for my water color effort depicting a baseball diamond, would have been proud. From the impressionists of Jeu de Paume, to every other European artist at the Louvre, to Chopin's birthplace and resting place, to Mozart's childhood home, to the great cathedrals of Vienna, Lausanne, and Paris, to palaces and castles, I was oozing culture from every pore. Absent Ewa

I would have never made the effort to take in half of what I saw that summer.

On August 17th we took the Metro to *Les Invalides*, a complex of museums dedicated to French military successes. The most cynical among you may question the need for more than one room, much less more than one building, to store relics of French military triumphs. Alas, you would be forgetting the exploits of "The Little Corporal," Napoleon Bonaparte, whose body is encased in a series of six coffins inside one very large sarcophagus. That sarcophagus rests at *Les Invalides* in a rotunda beneath the main dome of a chapel fashioned after Rome's St. Peter's Basilica. Aside from Napoleon's tomb, my most vivid memory of that day is the headline of the *Herald Tribune* newspaper: ELVIS PRESLEY DIES (or something to that effect). It was then I realized the global scope of "The King's" star power. Despite having grown up in Poland, Ewa knew all about Elvis.

Throughout the summer we had been discussing the particulars around our future. We had made several decisions. Ewa would make an encore visit to Iowa (subject to passport and visa approval) the next summer. I would return to Poland in two years, at which time we would marry. Following the wedding we would return together to the US, where we would establish our permanent home. We spent most of that final day in Paris reviewing the past ten weeks and trying our best to remain upbeat. This was now the third time I was going to say good-bye to this woman. At each parting the bond between us had grown stronger. To me she had progressed from cute tour guide, to exotic foreign girlfriend, to wife-to-be. I am not ashamed to tell you there were a few tears shed as we asked a passerby to take our photo at the airport. Today, when I watch the evening news and see the agonizing good-byes of couples, as one party heads off to an extended military hitch in some distant land, I can feel their anguish. Some turn around and walk away without looking back, as if they are ripping off the tape all at once, in an effort to get past the pain as quickly as possible. Others continue to wave, savoring the last glimpse, until the loved one is out of sight. With a final hug, I chose to "rip off the tape." I turned and walked down the jetway. It would be almost eleven months before we would see each other again.

August 19, 1977, at Orly Airport Paris, France:
The third time Tim and Ewa said good-bye until the next year

Chapter 7: Wedding Planner

The only communications I had had with anyone in the US during the summer of 1977 were the post card I sent from Gmunden, Austria (which had yet to arrive), and one phone call I had placed from Poland on the first day I had met Ewa's family. No one back home had yet learned of our engagement. My brother and his wife picked me up from Chicago upon my return the states. The six hour car ride back to Des Moines just flew by, as we had much to talk about. Steve and Laura were the first to learn of our wedding plans. I shared the information with the rest of the family during a picnic held to celebrate my arrival home.

My focus now turned to finding employment. Before leaving for Europe I had interviewed for a teaching position at Neil Armstrong Elementary School in Bettendorf, Iowa. I was told I was one of the two finalists for the position, but I did not get the job. I now had a fiancée and a $1500 loan balance, but I had no car and no income. Mom and Dad agreed to let me stay with them for a few months, but I was expected to pay a modest rent. I submitted applications to substitute teach with each of the school districts in the Des Moines area. I applied for the same bus driving position I had while attending Grand View College. I scoured the newspaper for any teaching position I could find.

Less than a week after my return I was called for an interview at a Catholic school in the tiny burg of Defiance, Iowa. The principal of the school offered me the job in the first five minutes of the interview. She told me my teaching duties would include one section of math, two sections of US history, and one period of health, in addition to all of the physical education. Oh yes, and could I teach just one section of religion? When I told her I wasn't even Catholic she dismissed it with, "but you are Christian, right?" I would be the basketball coach for both the boys and girls teams and I would drive the school bus every ninth week. I was to do all of this for the princely sum of eight thousand dollars per year. Though I would have no health insurance or retirement benefits, my daily hot lunch would be free. She assured me that as the lone male member of the ten-person faculty, the cooks would take special care of me. Since this was a Thursday and the school year was to start the following Monday, the principal had even taken the liberty of reserving and negotiating rent on a vacant furnished room—at the retirement home in the nearby town of Harlan!

I asked for twenty-four hours to decide. As I drove the seventy-five miles back to Des Moines I weighed the pros and cons. The cons: The salary was low, there were no retirement benefits, there was no health insurance, I would be teaching five different subjects, and I would be living in a retirement home. The pros: *It was a job*. I was within minutes of accepting the position when the phone rang. It was Earl Nevins, the man in charge of bus drivers for Saydel. He jokingly shared that I had survived the background check and had been cleared to drive the bus once again. I called the principal in Defiance and politely declined the teaching offer.

My plan was to drive the school bus and be a substitute teacher until I could land a permanent teaching job. I didn't wait very long. On the second day of school, the local middle school industrial arts teacher, Walt Crew (who had been my Driver's Education instructor eight years earlier), suffered a ruptured appendix. I was to be his replacement for the next month. This presented a logistics challenge for the school. I had just been hired to drive two bus routes in the morning and one in the afternoon, and was now the temporary shop teacher for some of the same students who were passengers on my route! The school's solve for this dilemma was to have another teacher take first period roll while I was parking my bus, and then to release me ten minutes early each day so I could retrieve my bus to take the students home. One day, one of the kids on the bus jokingly asked if I would prepare his lunch.

"Why do you ask?" I questioned.

"Well, you pick me up, drive me to school, teach me, and drive me home. I figure if you make my lunch you could be my dad."

While Mr. Crew was recovering from surgery one of the teachers at the high school abruptly decided to exit teaching. I was hired for a permanent position as soon as Mr. Crew returned to school. My duties included coaching responsibilities in tennis, baseball, and football. I would keep this position for the next ten years.

Ewa had started her own teaching career back in Poland. She had moved to Szczecin and accepted a position as an English instructor at the merchant marine academy there. Her students were the future officers of Poland's merchant marine fleet. She was earning extra money giving private English lessons. Her brother had also moved to Szczecin with his wife and son, leaving only her parents and her sister in Bydgoszcz.

We wrote weekly to each other, without fail, and quickly made plans for Ewa's return visit in the summer of 1978.

In late October, I read that President Carter was planning a visit to Iowa and was going to stay at the home of an Iowa farmer, Woody Diehl. The Diehl farm was about fifteen miles south of Des Moines.

I had many questions about the process of marrying someone from a communist country and thought I could cut through a bunch of red tape if I just wrote directly to the President and delivered the letter to the Diehls. After all, they were going to be seeing him pretty soon. The President was staying in their bedroom. Maybe they would hand him a personal note from Tim. I wordsmithed that letter about a dozen times before settling on the final draft. I was careful to sprinkle in some thinly-veiled compliments while asking for some personal guidance in the administrative journey in front of me and my Polish fiancée. I placed the letter in an envelope marked *President Carter: "Personal"* and drove to the Woody Diehl farm. My plan was to knock on the door, introduce myself, and personally ask Mr. Diehl to deliver the letter to President Carter on my behalf.

As I was circling the rural roads near Indianola in search of the Diehl farm, the absurdity of what I was about to do displaced my naiveté. I began to talk myself out of things.

"Think about what you are doing. Do you really think you are going to drive up to the farmhouse, knock on the door, hand these people a letter, and then ask them to give it to the President over scrambled eggs? Are you nuts?"

Then I answered back, "Why not? What's the worst that can happen? They can only tell you no."
The battle within continued.
"You're an idiot."
"So, you're a chicken."
"No, I'm not."
"Yes, you are."

I arrived at a compromise with myself. I decided to go home and place my letter to the President into another envelope addressed to the Diehls. I added a personal note requesting they share my letter with the President during his visit.

About a month after President Carter's visit I received a reply from the White House. The letter was signed by Hodding Carter III, Assistant Secretary of State for Public Affairs. Mr. Carter referenced a contact number in the State Department and suggested that I seek advice from them.

I called the number. After describing my situation to the lady from the State Department I asked for her opinion. She went on to explain the administrative complexities around legal status for non-resident alien spouses and sham marriages.

"Certainly it is possible for you to get married in Poland and bring your new wife into the US, but it would much easier to get married while your fiancée is visiting the US. If she will be in the US next summer and then will return to Poland for a year before you get married, then I think you should consider getting married while she is here. But, of course, that is your decision."

I shared the information with Ewa in my next letter. As I recall, she pretty much left the decision to me—perhaps one of the last times this has happened. The more I thought about it, the more I became convinced we should be married during her visit that summer. We agreed to go forward with this plan.

Grooms-to-be are blissfully ignorant of the wedding planning process. Most guys are already thinking about the honeymoon and just want to get past the traditional "first dance" at the reception. If you just tell the groom when to be at which church and the color of the tux he is to be wearing, he will rarely disappoint. He figures his work has been done. His creative energy has already been tapped in the pursuit of the woman of his dreams. He is more than willing to let the bride-to-be orchestrate the actual event. Heck, the bride's father is often underwriting the soiree and generally nothing is too good for his "Little Princess." The guy may even get a couple of free days with his buddies, while the fiancée is meeting with her posse to determine the appropriate shade of mauve to be used on the cocktail napkins. But alas, I was about to assume responsibilities of both bride and groom in preparation for our wedding—a task for which I was painfully ill-prepared.

Ewa's job was to secure a wedding dress. She had one custom made in Poland and it was beautiful. My job was... well, everything else. Mom was an invaluable resource for me. She provided a list of questions, the answers to which I was to obtain from Ewa. We needed to know her favorite color. (Blue). Did she prefer carnations or mums? (Carnations—and I later learned mums are traditional flowers at *funerals* in Poland). Chocolate or white cake? (White, but not too sweet). We needed names and addresses of friends and relatives in Poland to whom we should send invitations, and could any of them come for the wedding? It was important to include as many questions as possible in one letter because there was a three week turnaround for the response.

I chose the date, August 5th, because Central Lutheran Church was available. I talked with the Catholic Diocese to see if a Catholic priest would join the Lutheran minister in a joint ceremony. I found a photographer from an ad in the Highland Park Shopper. I asked my sister and Steve's wife to be bridesmaids. I gave Mom a list of guests to invite. She promptly doubled the number when Ewa replied that only one person from Poland could attend the wedding. I chose the color, design, and font for the invitations. I wanted to let Ewa make as many final choices as possible, but she was going to arrive just four weeks before the wedding, and many decisions had to be made prior to her arrival.

Of course, there were the traditional groom responsibilities as well. Marv, Scott, and my brother would stand up for me. Dad's barbershop quartet would sing the Lord's Prayer at the wedding. Dad and Kristi would also sing a duet. We would hold a rehearsal dinner at the Bavarian Haus Restaurant. We would go to Colorado on our honeymoon. Each day brought a new detail to be administered. I was beginning to think the lady at the State Department had miscalculated the complexities involved with a groom-planned US wedding and may have given me some poor advice.

In what can only be described as pure serendipity, Ewa's former roommate and my former tour guide, Maria Wołowska, was planning to visit friends and tour the US during the summer. She and a friend, Witold Marcinkowski, had been offered a car to use courtesy of an acquaintance in Ohio. Maria enthusiastically accepted Ewa's request to be her Maid of Honor. We were ecstatic to learn of Maria's participation in our ceremony. She had been the one who introduced us to one another in Poland and now she was to be in our wedding in Des Moines!

As Ewa was now teaching at the Maritime Academy she could not leave Poland until the end of June. We were less intimidated by the paperwork this time around and fortunately, Ewa again secured both a passport and visa. Before arriving in Des Moines she first visited New York City for a few days. She was hosted by a woman who had been to Poland as part of a group of international folk dance judges. Ewa had been her tour guide.

I went to the airport to meet Ewa on the weekend before the Fourth of July. It had been over ten months since we had last seen each other. She looked great but I noticed she was a little thin. I passed it off as the bride-to-be wanting to look her very best in her wedding gown. I must have been a little nervous because I ran the stoplight at East Sixth and Grand, where the offended driver immediately offered us the universal "single-digit salute" of contempt and a few choice words. Ewa was to stay with my parents until the wedding. I was living across town in an apartment with Marv Tuttle and another friend from high school, Steve Wolver.

The holiday was on a Tuesday so we had several days to get re-acquainted and to make some additional wedding arrangements before I had to work. During that weekend Ewa complained of being a little tired. We all assumed it was a combination of the excitement and travel fatigue until I made the observation that the whites of her eyes were not really white. They had a yellowish tint to them which seemed to match the new color of her tongue. Something wasn't right. Mom thought we should go to the hospital and have some tests run. I was a little hesitant to go because Ewa was not yet on my health insurance. We had gambled there would be no real need for health coverage for Ewa. She was only going to be here for two months and would return to Poland following our honeymoon.

It was the day before the holiday and the emergency room was the only real option. The doctor immediately ordered a blood test, the results of which were undeniable. Ewa had hepatitis! There are different strains of hepatitis and this was the least serious of them. To this day she is not certain how she contracted the disease, but given the incubation period she suspects it may have been during a dental procedure performed a week before her departure from Poland.

We had a thousand questions. "How serious is this? What is the treatment? Is it contagious? Will this disrupt the wedding?" The doctor took his time and calmly answered all of our queries. He wanted to put Ewa in the hospital for a few days, but conceded it would be possible for her to remain at home if she had no visitors and the house was clearly marked as "Quarantined." The only visitors to be allowed in the home were those who had already been in close contact with Ewa. Fortunately, I was in that select group. Unfortunately, those who had been exposed to the disease had to receive gamma globulin injections administered with needles whose circumference resembled roofing nails.

The doctor went on to explain, "Hepatitis is a disease that attacks the liver. Eat a lot of fresh fruits and vegetables. Stay away from fats, fried foods, and alcohol. No birth control pills. Something else. Blah, blah. Something else...."

I am certain there were a lot of additional very important instructions, but I didn't hear any of them. Once he got to the part about "no birth control pills," I stopped listening. This wasn't really happening was it? My fiancée, whom I hadn't seen in ten months, is diagnosed with a communicable illness two days after arriving in Des Moines. She is not covered under my insurance, so she is quarantined in my parents' home for the three weeks leading up to our wedding. No one is allowed to visit her except family members who receive special shots. Under no circumstances is she permitted to leave the house—even to attend our pre-marital counseling sessions with the Catholic priest and the Lutheran minister. Oh yeah, and she cannot take birth control pills while she is here.

We had been to our first marriage counseling session, with Pastor Stan Carlson, just a few hours before we went to the hospital where Ewa learned of her illness. Two days later, I alone returned to Pastor Carlson's office for the second—of our five—scheduled sessions. Naturally, I explained the reason for Ewa's absence and valiantly committed to continuing the process—though I had reservations as to the merits of single-participant marital counseling. I really didn't want to hear how I "should never leave the toilet seat up" unless she was there to hear that "it's not saving money if you buy two of something you really don't need just because it is on sale."

After about thirty minutes, Pastor Carlson looked at me and said, "Well, this really is kind of pointless. I guess if the two of you have gone to all of this trouble to be together, then I think you'll probably be okay. You don't have to continue with these sessions." Pastor Stan was a good guy.

Ewa's one requirement when she agreed to move the wedding to the summer of 1978, was to have the wedding recognized by the Catholic Church. When I was seventeen, I once attended Sunday Mass at a Catholic church with a former girlfriend. At the end of the mass the priest blessed my throat. This was the sum of my interaction with the Catholic Church in America before that summer. A month before Ewa's arrival I made several phone calls and was sent in the direction of Father David Polich, a young Catholic priest with shoulder-length hair. He consented to marry us in a joint service at the Lutheran church, provided we would attend pre-marital counseling sessions with him. It was now time for our first meeting.

Of course, I showed up at St. Joseph's Catholic Church minus my future wife. I could sense his disappointment. I believe he was genuinely looking forward to counseling us—as a couple. He was a part of a new ecumenical spirit where Catholics and Lutherans were celebrating their common backgrounds rather than focusing on their differences. We completed a first session and scheduled a second one. Five minutes into our second meeting he acknowledged that marital counseling is best done as a couple and, like Pastor Carlson, he relieved me of any obligation for future sessions.

In the days leading up to the wedding, friends and family would stop by Mom and Dad's house to wave to Ewa. I, too, would go to Mom and Dad's after work, but, having received the gamma globulin injection, I was allowed inside. During one of those visits I was sitting in the living room watching TV. Adjacent to the couch was an end table on which sat a blue Fostoria-like glass candy dish. I lifted the top and reached in for a piece of candy. Imagine my surprise when I discovered the dish was not filled with candy, but with condoms! I did a double take and began to laugh. I held one of the condoms in my hand and took it into the kitchen to confront my mother.

"Mom, what is this?" I asked in the most accusatory manner.
"Don't you know what that is?" she asked in shock.
"Of course I know what it is! I mean, why is it in the candy dish?!"

Her reply was clinical and delivered with all of the practicality befitting a mother and VD Nurse. "Well, I heard the doctor in the emergency room tell Ewa she could not use birth control pills at any time while she is here this summer. I didn't think she would want to get pregnant before returning to Poland. We give out free condoms at the clinic, and I thought you might have need for these, and I could save you some money."

Of course, she was correct on every point, but there is just something a little unnerving about your own mother pilfering a couple dozen condoms from the free clinic and leaving them in the candy dish, knowing full well you will accidentally discover them while sneaking a piece of candy. Nonetheless, I figured Mom knew best, so I made sure I grabbed a handful before leaving for my apartment.

It wasn't until the first of August that Ewa was free to leave the home and Mom and Dad were permitted to remove the "Quarantined" sign. Those last few days before the wedding were filled with trips to the jeweler, the photographer, the baker, and the florist for final preparations. Maria and Witold arrived in the middle of the week, in ample time to attend the wedding rehearsal and dinner.

I left Ewa at Mom and Dad's late Friday evening to return to my apartment, having agreed we would not see each other again until she walked down the aisle the next day. While driving home, I was stopped by a Johnston Police Officer for exceeding the posted speed limit. Though I have no hard evidence to support my hypothesis, I believe that pretty women are often afforded a leniency denied to men when they are suspected of a moving violation. On this occasion, however, I was released with just a warning after showing my marriage license and imploring the officer to give me an early wedding present. Even tough guy cops are suckers for things like that. I wondered if he secretly cried at "chick flicks" like I sometimes do.

Saturday August 5th, 1978 was warm and sunny. I had a bunch of loose ends to manage. I got the car washed and waxed. Chuck Knight, a friend and former school teacher at Saydel had agreed to let me park my car at his place during the day in an effort to keep it from being decorated. I went to the Pepper Tree Inn at the west edge of town and secured our room for the evening. I placed a call to the international operator to arrange a phone call to Ewa's parents. As I indicated earlier, a phone call to Poland required twelve to twenty four hours advance notice. I wanted the phone call to come to our hotel room around midnight (our time) on Saturday. This would be 7:00 AM Sunday morning in Poland. I needed to educate the hotel staff that an international operator would be calling our room sometime between 11:00 PM and 1:00 AM, and to please put the call through.

The wedding was at 7:00 PM and I decided to spend the afternoon at a high school all-star football game with Dave Dirksen and Brad Stolz. They were both teachers and coaches at Saydel and were to be the ushers at the wedding. The game was held at Drake Stadium and we feigned interest for a half before retiring to Peggy's, the local watering hole, for a beer. I think Brad and Dave were conspiring to get me drunk, but I stopped after my second beer.

As the Best Man it was Marv's job to get me to the church and make certain I had my tuxedo. We arrived about an hour before the ceremony. I, along with Scott, Marv, and my brother dressed in the lower level of the church and walked up the back stairs to the church sanctuary. We were to remain behind the side entrance until cued by the ushers to enter. As the four of us were waiting for the pre-arranged signal, I looked down at my shoes. A small piece of tape was stuck to the edge of one of them. As I reached down to remove the tape my groomsmen looked at each other and tried in vain to stifle collective laughter. I asked them what was so funny. I then looked at the sole of my left shoe, from which I had just removed a small piece of white adhesive tape. There I saw four or five more pieces of tape. I looked at my right shoe and saw even more tape. I looked back at my left shoe. By now all three of my groomsmen were laughing uncontrollably. Just as I began to figure out what was going on we got our cue to enter the sanctuary. Marv gently pushed me into the church and the others quickly followed.

The wedding had officially begun. First came Brad Stolz with my mother. They were followed by Laura, my sister, and Maria. The church was full, and all stood in unison as Ewa was escorted down the aisle by my father. My palms were sweating as I took Ewa's hand from Dad. The ceremony was proceeding as planned. Kristi and Dad sang a beautiful duet. Dad's quartet had never sounded so good as they shared *The Lord's Prayer*. Marv had remembered the rings. We exchanged vows and Ewa was particularly careful to enunciate all of the words correctly. The vows finished with the phrase, "according to God's holy ordinance." Kristi tells me Ewa had been practicing that phrase all morning, fearing she would not say it correctly. We had one final task before I could kiss the bride and be presented as husband and wife. We were to kneel, bow our heads, and accept the blessing. As the two of us knelt, I remembered the tape on my shoes. An audible, almost irreverent, murmur swept through the church as Pastor Carlson recited the blessing, and I knew why. The tape on the bottom of my left shoe formed the letters "H" and "E." On the right shoe were the letters "L" and "P." As we were receiving the blessing all in attendance were reading "HELP" on the bottom of my shoes. That's why the guys had been laughing as we waited to enter the sanctuary. I had forgotten about my shoes until I heard the whispering during the blessing.

I was finally allowed to kiss the bride as Pastor Carlson announced to all in attendance, "I now present to you, Mr. and Mrs. STEVE PRATT."

Yes, Stan Carlson had presided over Steve and Laura's wedding two years earlier, but c'mon Stan. I turned back to Pastor Carlson and corrected him. He quickly hit the rewind button and presented us again. This time he got it right and we briskly recessed the church to applause and smiles.

Check out the shoes: "H-E-L-P," courtesy of the best man

Our reception was a very modest cake and punch affair held at the church. It was followed by a smaller reception at Mom and Dad's home where several aunts and friends had helped to prepare the food in advance. These certainly were not the lavish doings of a traditional Polish wedding, but it was what we could afford.

As our friends and family gathered on the front lawn to send us off to our first night of wedded bliss, I could not find my car keys. I was convinced Marv or Scott had taken my keys in a sophomoric effort to delay our honeymoon. As we sat in the car pleading for the return of my keys a young cousin continued to pelt me with rice while another was decorating the back window with shaving cream. (So much for hiding the car throughout the day). I was becoming more and more agitated. Marv and Scott insisted they had not taken my keys. I began to raise my voice and started to swear, when Kristi mercifully intervened.

"I found the keys. They were on the nightstand in the bedroom." Apparently I had emptied my pockets when I changed out of my tuxedo. This was one of those moments for which I needed a "mulligan," you know, a "do over." I had just made a complete ass of myself at my own wedding reception. Fortunately, I had the good sense to apologize to Ewa within minutes of having squealed away in my powerful Toyota sub compact. I will take this opportunity to offer my sincerest apologies to all who witnessed my boorish behavior.

Sometimes I read where couples, to celebrate a specific anniversary, will return to the place where they spent their wedding night. If we were to do that it would require the temporary displacement of some administrative personnel employed by the Polk County branch of the Iowa State University Extension Office. The university acquired the Pepper Tree Inn more than twenty years ago. "Our" room is now occupied by people who help farmers increase their soybean yield. But on August 5th, 1978, it is where we spent the first night as Mr. and Mrs. Steve...er...pardon me...Tim Pratt. The more intimate details will be left to your imagination, but I can tell you we received a phone call from the front desk around 12:30 AM. It was the call which I had previously arranged. Ewa was confirming, in Polish of course, she was now Mrs. Pratt and was answering the many questions about the wedding. The connection was not good and Ewa had to raise her voice to be heard. This apparently disturbed the occupants of the adjacent room because there were two slaps against the wall followed by some muffled tones, which I interpreted as an indication we might have awakened them. I wanted to yell back that it was my wedding night and we could make noise if we wanted, but I thought better of it.

Before departing Des Moines the next morning we headed for a car wash to remove the decorations from the previous evening. I failed to lower the car antenna and it was broken off by the automatic machine as we drove through it. My car had no tape player and now we had no radio. Our destination for the first night was North Platte, Nebraska, as it was about halfway to our ultimate destination in Silverthorne, Colorado.

Without a radio we were forced to design our own entertainment. We sang. My wife's talents are many, and I have shared but a few with you to this point, but perfect pitch is not among them. Neither is relative pitch. "He couldn't carry a tune with a wicker basket," is a favorite phrase of my father, as he describes the musically-challenged. He would never say this about Ewa, though he might think it. I convinced Ewa to practice during our trip. I promised not to make fun of her and so we sang for a couple of hours to pass the time.

Marv Tuttle's aunt and uncle, Millie and Lowell Troester, lived in Brighton, Colorado. They owned a cabin in Silverthorne located about 100 miles west of Denver in the Rockies. Marv, Scott, and I had stayed there on a post-high school trip a few years earlier. They had agreed to rent the cabin to Ewa and me for our honeymoon. We stopped in Brighton to pick up the keys and drove on to Silverthorne. The cabin was situated on the Blue River at what was then the northern-most edge of town. (Several years later, while returning from a skiing trip to Steamboat Springs, we located the cabin. It is now toward the southern end of town and serves as a combination hardware store and bait shop). A year earlier we had been hitchhiking in the Alps of Switzerland staying at youth hostels. Now, we were in our own car, cruising the Rocky Mountains, and happy to be the lone occupants in this beautiful setting.

The cabin had beds for twelve persons, but we had opted against inviting friends to our honeymoon. There was a fireplace, too. My boyhood home didn't have one of those, and I had received no formal training in fireplace fundamentals. As night began to fall, so too, did the temperature. I retrieved some wood from the stack outside, placed it in the fireplace, and managed to somehow initiate a fire without betraying my inexperience at this task. We huddled close together for warmth—this was, after all, our honeymoon. Just as things started to "heat up," both literally and figuratively, smoke began to fill the room. I had to fill a pot with water to douse the flames. We opened the door to air out the cabin. We were coughing and our eyes were watering. Ewa asked if I had opened the flue.

"The what?" I asked.

"The flue. Didn't you open the flue?" she queried again.

"No. I couldn't find the switch. Where's the flue? What's a flue?" I protested.

"You can't be serious! You started a fire in the fireplace without opening the flue?!"

It was more a statement than a question. She began to laugh because her alternative was to cry. This was merely the prelude to a series of my shortcomings which would reveal themselves over the next thirty years (I once paid the appliance repairman forty dollars, only to have him show me the reset button on my garbage disposal). Poor Ewa. It was too late to back out now. She had accepted me "for better or for worse," but she was hardly anticipating the extent of my ineptitude at mechanical tasks.

We took day trips to Glenwood Springs, Estes Park, and Aspen, returning to our cabin in Silverthorne each evening. We went to Cave of the Winds and stayed a night in Colorado Springs, en route to Hutchinson, Kansas. Hutchinson was the home of Helen Stone, a delightful woman who was Ewa's acquaintance from one of the tourist groups she had hosted in Poland. From Hutchinson we made our way to Kansas City and finally returned to Des Moines. As a concession to our fond memories of the previous summer's travels we even picked up a hitchhiker just north of Kansas City, depositing him at the I-80 turn off on the west edge of Des Moines.

Upon our return to Des Moines we had less than a week before Ewa was to fly back to Poland. This was barely enough time to open our wedding gifts and for Ewa to pack. Damn, that drive to the airport was tough, but the drive home was even tougher. Two-a-day football practices were starting and served to occupy my thoughts during the day, but sleeping with a football isn't the same as sleeping with your new wife.

Chapter 8: It's Hard to Argue from 5,000 Miles Away

During our first year of marriage we exchanged dozens of letters, a few telegrams, and about four phone calls. Ewa was teaching at the Maritime Academy in Szczecin and busy administering the final details for her permanent immigration to the US. Among those details was a three year work obligation required of all college graduates in Poland at the time. Once Ewa had passed the very rigorous college entrance exams, her schooling had been free. Any failure to fulfill the work obligation would require a repayment of the cost of the education. She had worked one year prior to our wedding and was now in the second year of that responsibility. She had no plans to complete the third year, as she was immigrating to the US. This meant we had to repay the Polish government one third of the cost for her college education. Here we turned once more to the "black market." I sent cash (about $1,500-$2,000, I think) with a friend who was going to Poland. She used the money to pay off the school obligation, purchase her own diamond engagement ring, and to buy as much crystal as the funds would allow. Ewa was granted a one-time exemption from export duty on all of her worldly possessions because she was leaving the country to legally immigrate to the US.

The plan was for Ewa to secure passage on one of the merchant ships operated by the Polish Steamship Company. The graduates of Maritime Academy generally went straight to the Polish Steamship Company as officers. As an academy professor, Ewa would receive a discount on the ticket and she would have no luggage weight restrictions. I was going to remain in the US and meet her wherever, and whenever, her ship came to port. Most all of my spare money had been sent to Poland and we agreed that I should not spend the money to go to Poland. My parents thought otherwise. Mom felt it was absolutely necessary that I go to Poland.

Mom made the case: "Your wife is leaving her parents and leaving her country. I can only imagine how difficult this must be for her parents.

You need to go there to be with your wife and to reassure her parents that you will take care of her." Of course I wanted to go to Poland, but the long-distance nature of our relationship had strained our budget.

It was late April when Mom and Dad announced they wanted to give me an early birthday present (my birthday is May 22nd). They presented me with a one-way plane ticket to Poland. This became a running joke in our family. In 1979, there probably weren't too many people from the US flying "to" any communist country on a "one way" ticket. In fact, the ticket was to Berlin, as this was the closest major international airport to Szczecin. The travel itinerary was brutal: Des Moines to Chicago. Chicago to New York. New York to Frankfurt. Frankfurt to West Berlin. West Berlin airport (Tegel) to East Berlin train station via the U-bahn, where one was required to disembark and travel through a checkpoint into East Germany. Re-board the U-bahn to the train station in East Berlin, and finally take the train from East Berlin to Szczecin. Nonetheless, I was ecstatic and, after profusely thanking my parents, immediately sent a telegram to Ewa.

Several years ago a friend gave my wife a coffee mug with the inscription, "Three Reasons to Become a Teacher: June, July, and August." Even though most teachers would argue they generally take summer jobs to supplement their teaching salaries, they would also concede that having summers free is a nice perk. I was going to take maximum advantage of this benefit. The students had completed their year on Thursday May 31st. The staff reported on the following day to turn in their grades, staplers, and tape dispensers. I left school and drove straight to the airport.

Ewa had asked me to bring as many empty suitcases as possible. While she had not accumulated too many worldly possessions, she was packing for more than just a trip. She was moving to a different country. I was instructed to include a bare minimum of clothes in a backpack and to bring a large suitcase filled with a series of smaller suitcases. That is what I did…well, almost.

Lola Bobolinski immigrated with her parents and siblings to the US from Poland in the late 1960s, when she was in her teens. I met her in the fall of 1975, after returning from my initial visit to Poland. I had been eager to learn the language and to meet anyone from Poland. I wanted to share my experiences and to learn as much as I could about the country, its culture, and its history. Lola (her real name was Leonarda) and I had become friends. I introduced Lola to Ewa when she first came here in 1976. Lola frequently traveled back to her native Poland, and unbeknown to me, was married while in Poland in the summer of 1978. In fact, she and her new husband, Waldemar Darowski, were married on the exact same day as Ewa and me! She had gone to Poland in 1978 with the express intent of marrying Waldek. Administrative red tape (the very kind of thing about which I had been warned by the lady from the State Department) had caused a couple of delays to their late June wedding date, pushing their wedding day to August 5th. Following their honeymoon in Poland, Lola returned to the US while Waldek remained in Poland. Really, how strange is that?! Lola married a guy in Poland and returned to the US without him. Ewa married me and returned alone to Poland. I was living here without my wife and Lola was living here without her husband. We even determined that Ewa and Lola had crossed paths in the air as they each returned to their respective countries on the same day. Waldek had left Poland permanently in early May, 1979, to come and live with his wife. Now, a few weeks later, I was headed to Poland to retrieve my wife.

The night before I was to leave, Lola and Waldek visited me and asked that I courier a package to Poland and mail it as soon as I got there. This was kind of like a pre-Federal Express high priority service. At that time, first class delivery of international parcels would take ten days, on average, to arrive. Since I would be in Poland in less than thirty-six hours, I could mail the parcel in Poland and it would arrive at its final destination at least a week in advance of any other postal service delivery. They gave me the package, which was a plain small cardboard box secured with packing tape. It had been addressed. They gave me a couple of dollars for the postage I was to purchase as soon as I got to Poland. Lola gave me a list of the package contents: some panty hose, a jar of peanut butter, and few other consumer items which were hard to come by in Poland. I placed the package inside of a suitcase, which was inside another suitcase, which was inside yet another suitcase, and thought nothing more of it.

The flight to Chicago was uneventful, but JFK was backed up and we circled for almost two hours. I was certain I would miss the plane to Frankfurt. As I exited the aircraft at JFK I walked immediately to the departures sign. My connecting gate was the very next gate. I doubt that could happen today as most international flights arrive and depart from a separate terminal. All was fine at Frankfurt and I made the transfer to Berlin without incident. Now came the hard part. I took the U-bahn (the metro rail system in Berlin) and headed in the direction of the Lichtenberg Train Station in East Berlin, where I was to catch the train to Szczecin. This route crossed from West Berlin into East Berlin. All passengers were required to disembark the train and pass through a border patrol checkpoint at Friedrichstrasse, also known as Checkpoint Charlie.

As you may well know, following World War II, the city of Berlin and the country of Germany were divided into four zones of occupation representing the four major Allied nations (France, England, USA, and the Soviet Union). The British, French, and American sectors of the country became West Germany and the Soviet section became East Germany. Berlin was divided in much the same way. However, the city of Berlin lies entirely inside of what was East Germany. In 1961, the Soviets constructed a wall around West Berlin isolating its citizens from the rest of the world. The purpose of The Wall was to stop East Berliners from traveling freely to West Berlin where they would often remain. West Berliners were free to travel to East Berlin, needing only their passports to return home. East Berliners were rarely permitted to leave their zone.

I appeared to be the lone non-commuter, non-Berliner on the U-bahn that day. Descending the steps from the platform at the Friedrichstrasse stop I found myself at the end of a long line of people waiting to have documents checked. I was the only person with a backpack. I was the only person carrying a suitcase and a shoulder bag. I would have been less conspicuous with a scarlet letter emblazoned on my forehead. It felt as if everyone was staring at me only because everyone was. As if to prove my point, two uniformed guards motioned for me to step away from the line and to follow them. They led me to a separate counter near to where the other passengers were having their documents checked.

The two guards asked me a few things in German, to which I replied, "Ich verstehe Sie nicht." ("I don't understand you"). Here's a tip should you ever find yourself in a similar situation: Do not tell a border guard you don't understand his language and his questions while speaking to him in his native language. He will either believe you to be a smart ass, or he will ask even more questions in his native tongue, further elevating the tension you are experiencing.

As one guard reviewed my documents, the second one emptied my backpack. He removed the entire contents of the pack—even my underwear. Both were fascinated with my little pocket instamatic camera and accompanying flash cubes. But if they were fascinated by the camera and flash cubes, they were completely vexed when they opened my big suitcase to find only another suitcase. This apparently aroused some suspicion because two more uniformed sorts, one of whom was a woman—were summoned. Together they opened the inner suitcase to discover yet another suitcase. By now, the line of commuters waiting to show their documents was equally interested in the contents of my suitcases. The four guards together opened my final suitcase, which revealed the cardboard box I was transporting for Lola.

The female guard asked me a question in German, which I assumed was something on the order of, "What is in the package?"

I smiled and said, "Panty hose, peanut butter, and a bunch of other stuff." She took the box to a little area behind the counter where there appeared to be small x-ray machine. The guards huddled together and then sought guidance from yet another woman. At that moment I began to take inventory of the situation. Here I was as the lone, middle-of-the-day, non-local commuter, at a subway station in Communist East Berlin, with a backpack, three empty suitcases, and a non-descript brown cardboard box as luggage. Even I had to admit it looked a little strange. But I was not anticipating what happened next.

The second woman came out to address me in English, which was burdened by an accent similar to that of the little boy who saved me on the train two years earlier.

"*Ant zir, pleez tell me uhnt vy do yoo haf a gun*? ("And Sir, please tell me why do you have a gun?").
"A what?!" was my reply.
"*A gun, a peestolet, a gun. Bang! Bang!*" ("A gun, a pistol. Bang! Bang!"). Here she cocked her thumb and pointer finger at me and fired her imaginary weapon, simultaneous to the words "Bang! Bang!"
"I don't have a gun! Go ahead, open the package. You will see. You are crazy. Of course, I don't have a gun." I must confess, for one very brief instant I thought to myself, "Lola wouldn't have put a gun in there would she? Nah, she would have said something. The parcel is too small, anyway. They are just messing with you."

I was now certain the package did not contain a gun or they would have done something to me. Had I been a few years younger, or had this been my first experience with East European border control agents, I might have panicked. Instead, I leaned against the counter and smiled politely at the passing commuters as they gawked at me and my underwear. After about fifteen minutes one of the male guards came out and motioned I could go. I quickly jammed my clothes into the backpack, put the suitcases inside of one another, and went up the steps to catch the next train to Lichtenberg Station.

I had five hours before the train was to depart, no East German currency, and my day had started some twenty-two hours earlier at Saydel High School. I was beat and it was hot. All of the benches on the platform were occupied, so I positioned my backpack against one of the support poles and sat down to lean against it. My plan was to keep a very low profile and to try and rest some before my train came, though I really didn't want to fall completely asleep.

Several trains came and went and I ignored the obvious glances being thrown my way. After about three hours a train much longer than the others pulled up to the platform. This train had overnight compartments and a dining car. The train came to rest with the dining car positioned directly in front of where I was leaning against my backpack. I looked up to see six early-twenties macho-types, each with a cigarette in one hand and a *bier* in the other, staring at me as they leaned out the dining car windows. This was clearly not their first round of drinks and they wanted to have some fun.

"Hey, Yahnkee, [something... something] *arbeit* [...something...]," followed by a group howl of laughter. The only word I understood was *arbeit* (work) because the phrase "*Arbeit Macht Frei*" (Work will make you free) is written above the entrance to Auschwitz. I thought it best to simply re-adjust my backpack, face the other way, and ignore them.

This worked for about two minutes until a bottle cap landed next to me. I ignored it. Then a second one and a third one. The smart choice was to gather my things and move to the other end of the platform. But this was now an East meets West kind of unspoken challenge. I felt a deep sense of nationalist exuberance coupled with a need to defend my honor. I switched my backpack to the original position and assumed my place seated on the platform. I looked straight at the lot of them. There were no more bottle caps, but they began making little comments to one another and laughing among themselves. So, I made some none-too-polite comments and occasionally laughed as well. I'm certain I looked like a total fool because I was talking only to myself and then laughing at my own comments. At least when they said something it was to somebody else. This ridiculous charade, where none of us understood what the other was saying but each of us felt superior for having said it, went on for three or four minutes before the conductor announced the train's departure. I was glad to see it pull away from the station.

The distance from Berlin to Szczecin is only about eighty miles, but this train made three or four stops in between. I was fading in and out of sleep and was afraid I might miss Szczecin. That concern was totally unjustified because the final stop was Szczecin and we had two sets of border controls before arriving. East German passport control agents checked our documents at the Polish border. Then we traveled about one hundred feet and Polish agents checked our documents.

It was late in the evening when we finally reached Szczecin's central train station. Though thoroughly exhausted from the thirty-hour, Des Moines-New York-Frankfurt-West Berlin-East Berlin-Szczecin journey, I remember thinking that this was "it." No, "it" was not the finish line. "It" was that final big hill in the long-distance race. You know, the one where if you reach its peak you know everything is going to be fine. The one where you know you still have a ways to go, but from which you are now certain you will finish. Would she be there? She just *had* to be there. It was very dark and if there were lights at this end of the platform they needed to be replaced. As I exited the train I honestly could not tell if the depot was to the right or to the left I took about five steps in what turned out to be the wrong direction....

Then behind me I heard, "Tim, is that you?" I knew it was Ewa. "Yes, honey. It's me, but I can't see you."

As I turned to walk toward the voice, I squinted to make out her profile. I took off my backpack and placed my suitcases and shoulder bag on the ground. I hugged my wife for the first time in ten months. I had made it up that final hill. No, *we* had made it up that final hill. At that moment I knew I could finish the race. We pledged to never do this separation thing again. And we haven't.

Chapter 9: Second Honeymoon

Ewa had been provided housing by the Maritime Academy as a benefit of her employment. It was a tiny dormitory room near to the school and not far from the central train station. This was to be our home for the next few weeks as we made the final preparations for our journey back to the US. There were so many details to be administered. Fortunately, detail administration is yet another of Ewa's heretofore unlisted talents. First, we went to a carpenter and had him construct two large solid wood pine crates to hold non-clothing items. We bought our tickets for the ship that would return us across the Atlantic. There were special papers to be signed. There were more items to be purchased. Think of packing to move, not packing for a trip. Dishes, silverware, fine china (Ewa's family had given us a beautiful china service for twelve as our wedding gift; thirty years later it still adorns our dining room table for every special occasion), jewelry, pots, pans, knick knacks, and photo albums—each item carefully wrapped and labeled by Ewa. Then came customs inspections, complete with a bottle of fine cognac as our personal "thank you" to the officer who sealed our crates after approving their contents. (Apparently there was a limit on the amount of crystal which could be exported duty free, even if one was emigrating. Hence the cognac).

Shortly after my arrival, Ewa took me on a farewell tour to visit relatives. This included some friends and cousins in Bydgoszcz and her maternal grandmother's home in the city of Radom. *Babcia Fela* (Babcia is "grandmother" in Polish) was an interesting character. Well into her eighties when I met her, she was full of advice for the American husband of her granddaughter. "Treat her well. Never go to bed angry with one another. It is OK to drink, but not too much." As if to confirm her words delivered around the breakfast table, she pulled out a bottle of *Miodówka*, (homemade honey vodka) with two large *kieliszki* (something akin to shot glasses). She filled both shot glasses to the top and smiled at me. Raising the glass she looked me in the eye and said, "*Na zdrowie i sto lat*" ("To your health and may you live 100 years"). Then in one very swift motion she knocked back that double shot of vodka. I am a modest social drinker more partial to beer and wine than to hard liquor, but this had the feel of a rite of passage. I had to participate. It was as if she was giving me the seal of approval into the family. If this eighty year old matriarch could put away a vodka shot at 10:00 AM, I sure as heck wasn't about to wimp out. I tossed back my *kieliszek* and exhaled as if this was something I did every day. Of course, the closest I had ever come to consuming alcohol at that time of the morning was Sunday communion—and communion had never followed a breakfast of strawberry compote and strawberry *naleśniki* (similar to pancakes) covered with strawberry jam.

Strawberries (*truskawki*) are a seasonal treat and are generally served as such. However, they become a staple of the diet when they are the only food items in the stores. You see, while we were visiting Babcia Fela in Radom, another tourist—someone of far greater interest to most Poles—was roaming southern Poland. Pope John Paul II was on his first pilgrimage to Poland since becoming Pope in October 1978. (His predecessor, Pope John Paul I, died after only thirty-three days as Pope, amid some very questionable circumstances. Conspiracy theorists continue to have a field day with this subject). Think Times Square at midnight on New Year's Eve. Now multiply times three or four. This was the amoeba-like mass of humanity that followed the Pontiff's every move for nine days in June of 1979. Food and other consumer items were diverted from stores in cities like Radom to cities where the Pope was holding daily mass. Meat, potatoes, and vegetables had disappeared from the shelves, forcing Babcia Fela to reach deep into her culinary bag of tricks. Apparently my penance for not going to see His Holiness in person was to eat strawberries at every meal for three straight days. I made a mental note to make an effort to see the Pope if I ever got this close to him again.

We returned to Szczecin. Of course, we had to have a wedding celebration. Ewa's siblings and their spouses and her parents joined us at the Kaskada Restaurant. This was among the finest in all of Szczecin. (Several years later the Kaskada was destroyed by fire and was never rebuilt). We had a grand time. Dinner, drinks, dancing, and a variety show (which finished with the requisite striptease) were included. Thanks, once again, to that "underground economy," the total bill for the evening was less than fifty dollars.

In the middle of June we learned our departure date from Szczecin would be July 1st aboard the freighter, *General Madalinski*. (General Antoni Madalinski was a Polish military hero who lived in the late 1700s). Szczecin is the largest port, in terms of cargo tonnage, on the Baltic Sea, but it is about forty miles from the open water. It is connected to the sea by way of a river and a bay. It opens to the Baltic Sea at the town of Świnoujście. Having said our very emotional good-byes we boarded on July 1, 1979, as the lone passengers on a cargo ship loaded with coal. Our first stop was to be Rouen, France, where we would discharge the coal. The itinerary indicated about two days in France, and then we would cross the Atlantic Ocean to New Orleans, Louisiana. There, the *General Madalinski* would fill its massive holding bins with sulphates before returning to Poland. Prior to leaving for Poland that summer Mom and Dad had told me they would come to meet our ship at its final destination to help us transport our luggage. I sent a telegram to my parents informing them of our approximate date of arrival in New Orleans.

The cargo is priority one on a merchant vessel. Paying passengers are a bonus. For this reason any passenger on a freighter must have a flexible schedule. Ewa didn't have a job and my football practice wasn't scheduled to begin until the middle of August. We were told that two weeks would probably be sufficient time to reach our anticipated final destination in New Orleans. Time was an abundant commodity for us, or so we thought.

Our stateroom cabin consisted of a large living room with an executive desk, a bar, two arm chairs, a couch, and a large coffee table. Adjacent to the living room was our bedroom and bathroom. It wasn't until about twelve years later, when we went on our first passenger cruise, that we realized our freighter accommodations had been about four times the size of a standard cabin on a cruise ship.

As the only fare-paying passengers aboard the ship we were treated as celebrities. We were assigned a personal steward whose job it was to clean our room, refresh our linens, and cater to our every whim. We were invited to dine with the captain and the first officer. We were introduced to the chief engineer and the second and third officers. Two of the younger officers immediately recognized Ewa as their English instructor at the Maritime Academy. We learned the captain, Piotr Nowakowski, and the first officer were avid bridge players. On several occasions we were invited to the captain's quarters for bridge marathons which extended well into the night. We were given personal guided tours of the captain's bridge, where I was permitted to steer the ship on the high seas for a very brief moment. The chief engineer took us deep into the bowels of the vessel to observe the very loud engines. We visited the huge holding bins, which were as deep as a five story building. We could request any food item from the ship's galley at any time of the day or night. If there was no one on duty to prepare something, we were free to roam the kitchen and raid the refrigerator. This was the way to travel!

Once on a family trip to St. Paul, Minnesota, when I was about seven years old, I fell into the water of the little boat ride at the Como Park Zoo. Excluding the thirty minutes on Gray's Lake in Des Moines, when I rented a paddle boat—you know, the kind where you pedal for all you're worth and never really go anywhere—with an old girlfriend, the Como Park incident was the sum of my sea-faring experience prior to the General Madalinski. This was different. This was educational. This was interesting. It was fascinating. And... I was sharing it with my wife.

Have you ever wondered what a merchant seaman does all day while at sea? I'll tell you. He cleans the ship. He paints the ship. He works on general maintenance items. When his shift is done he plays cards, or ping pong, or foosball. (Don't ever bet against a sailor in a ping-pong tournament, unless maybe he is up against a Chinese guy. If the Chinese guy is also a sailor then bet the farm). He probably has a beer or two and maybe listens to some music. If it is Wednesday or Saturday he might even go to one of the movies in the ship's meeting room. He always checks the sky and the horizon. I am convinced that my local TV weatherperson would be far more accurate with his forecasts if he simply spent a summer on a merchant ship on the open water. I dare say this would cost the TV station considerably less money, and yield noticeably better results, than the acquisition of the newest super-duper Doppler radar technology.

The trip from Swinoujście to LeHavre, France, was about three days, as I recall. The journey took us out to the Baltic Sea, north around the tip of Denmark, and then southwesterly down through the English Channel to Le Havre. Here the ship was met by a local sea pilot who guided us the final fifty miles up the Seine River to Rouen. This was another new experience for me. At certain points on the way to Rouen, our ship seemed to take up almost the entire expanse of the Seine. We were displacing a significant amount of water. The homes and the people along the river's banks were close enough we could talk to them without yelling. I wondered how deep the water had to be to support a ship carrying 35,000 tons of coal. After several hours we pulled up to the main unloading dock where the ship was secured. We were told it would take two to three days to discharge the coal. During the time in port we were free to come and go as we pleased. Meals would be served on the ship, but we did not have to check in for forty-eight hours. We thought about catching a train for a quick return to Paris, but decided instead to explore Rouen with several members of the crew.

Rouen is the home of another Notre Dame Cathedral, again not to be confused with "The" Notre Dame Cathedral of Paris, or the Cathedral of Notre Dame in Lausanne, Switzerland, or the Fighting Irish of South Bend, Indiana. Like most cathedrals bearing this name, it is an architectural marvel of immense beauty. Rouen also is where the nineteen year-old, Joan of Arc, was burned at the stake in 1431. She had led the French in several remarkable military triumphs against British forces in the Hundred Years War. Joan had been captured in a battle by some British sympathizers and sold to the British. She had claimed divine guidance in the form of some visions and voices as explanation for her military prowess. These claims led to a conviction on the crime of heresy, and she was sentenced to death.

As we returned to the ship the chief engineer, who was in our group, noticed the huge overhead cranes, which were used in unloading of the coal, were not moving. He said this was very strange. Apparently when a cargo ship is in port the cranes are manned around the clock. We looked up and down the piers and observed none of the cranes were moving at any of the other ships, as well. As we boarded the vessel we learned that the longshoremen had gone on strike while we were in town. No one had any idea as to when they might return to work. This meant we were stranded in Rouen, France, aboard a floating hotel where we would be served four meals a day. We were absent the casinos, stage shows, and multiple lounges of a cruise ship, but we were not complaining.

The captain organized a bus tour of the area, complete with a guide to explain the history of the region. We even visited a home that had something to do with the French author, Victor Hugo (*Les Miserables*, *The Hunchback of Notre Dame*). I always thought it was one of his boyhood residences, but I can find no record that he actually lived in the area near Rouen. So, I am not certain whose house we visited. Personally, I was hoping the tour would take us to the beaches of Normandy to see the place where the Allies opened the second front in Europe on June 6, 1944, but the distance was too great for the day tour. Each morning after breakfast we would walk to the nearest bus stop and go into Rouen. While we were passing the days in Rouen I learned about a little bike race the French host each year, *Le Tour de France*. It had passed near Rouen and Le Havre a few days earlier and we would have had time to catch a glimpse of it. Honestly, I knew almost nothing about the event at the time. I regret my ignorance because *Le Tour* was won that year by the legendary Bernard Hinault. Hinault won the race five times and prior to the exploits of one Lance Armstrong, Mr. Hinault was considered the greatest of all bike racers. We were docked in Rouen for Bastille Day, July 14th. Bastille Day is to France what the Fourth of July is to the United States. There were celebrations in Rouen, but it was a cool, cloudy, rainy day. We opted to return to the ship when one of the crew members repeated a rumor that the strike had ended. Privately, I doubted the strike would have been called off during a holiday, but I kept that opinion to myself. I was feeling a little under the weather and was glad we returned to the ship. As I recall, we ended up just staying on the ship that day.

After about seven or eight days, and almost as if the French Longshoremen's Union knew my pre-season football schedule, the workers called an end to their strike. In less than thirty-six hours, the *General Madalinski* was making its way along the Seine and back to Le Havre and the Atlantic Ocean. There was just one problem: Captain Nowakowski had not been told where we were going. While we had been docked in Rouen waiting out the strike, the Polish Steamship Company had dispatched a different ship to New Orleans to take on the sulphates. We were simply to begin our journey across the ocean and "await further instructions."

The Captain assured us that we could use the ship's radio communications to call my parents once he received his orders. He plotted a course across the North Atlantic and "awaited further instructions." He received those instructions in the middle of the night and informed us at breakfast. We were now headed to Port Cartier, Canada, to be loaded with grain. After breakfast Captain Nowakowski took us to the bridge so we could locate Port Cartier on a map. Port Cartier is some three hundred and fifty miles northeast of Quebec on the north shore of the St. Lawrence River and about *one thousand six hundred miles* from Des Moines, Iowa. The captain told us we would enter the St. Lawrence River along the coast of the Canadian provinces of Newfoundland and Labrador and we should arrive in Port Cartier in about four days!

There we were: two twenty-four year olds, with eleven suitcases, two crates, and most of our worldly possessions, aboard a freighter, somewhere in the North Atlantic Ocean, bound for a very small Canadian port located over twenty-five hundred miles from where I had last told my parents we would arrive—and we would be there in less than four days. This was our situation as we went to the communications room to meet with the radio officer, who was to assist us in placing a call to my parents.

Radar O' Reilly of MASH is one of my favorite all-time television characters, and not just because he hailed from Ottumwa, Iowa. He was a resourceful chap who did what he could in some difficult situations. I remember several MASH episodes where Radar rang up Sparky, who patched him through to Seoul, and then on to Tokyo, before finally getting through to Mill Valley, California, for B.J. to talk with Peg—or to Maine for Hawkeye to tell his father he wasn't really dead—or back to Indiana so Henry Blake could help Lorraine balance her checkbook. Well, this is exactly what I felt like when the radio officer took a microphone (eerily similar to the one Radar used) and placed a call to someone on another ship, who then forwarded us on to yet another voice. I was asked to repeat my parents' phone number while facing a wall of communication equipment. A few buzzes were followed by some static and then I heard a phone ringing. The voice on the other end was undeniably my father's.

"Hello."

"Dad, this is Tim."

"Where are you?"

"Somewhere in the middle of the Atlantic Ocean."

"Helen, it's Tim. He is somewhere in the Atlantic Ocean. I'll ask him when he's coming to New Orleans. Tim, when will you be in New Orleans? We'll come to meet you. Just tell us when to be there."

"Dad, that's why I'm calling. We are not coming to New Orleans. It's a long story, but we are coming to Canada instead."

"That's great! Canada is even closer."

"No, Dad. You better get a map."

"Just tell us where and when and we will be there."

"Dad, get a map. The place is Port Cartier and it is way up the St. Lawrence River. It is several hundred miles beyond Quebec. Are you sure you can come? We will be there in just over three days. It is a very long way from Des Moines."

"It's no problem. I have time off from work and we will be there."

What I didn't know at the time was that my father had just had some knee surgery and had time off to recuperate. I gave him the name of the ship and told him we would continue the conversation in a few days. This would be our only chance to talk before our arrival in Port Cartier. Keep in mind this was long before cell phones, and ships did not have area codes followed by seven digit phone numbers. When we hung up, or signed off, really, Ewa asked me if I honestly thought they would be there when we arrived. I told her I wasn't so sure, but I certainly hoped so.

Even during mid-summer, the North Atlantic Ocean can offer up some pretty unforgiving conditions. We endured frigid winds, sleet, and rolling swells as Captain Nowakowski guided us toward North America. The Captain warned we might encounter an iceberg or two along the way, though I don't recall actually seeing one. The ship was equipped with a small holding tank, which the crew referred to as their swimming pool. In warmer climates, the "pool" was occasionally filled with ocean water to offer a respite from the intense heat of the sun. Our change in destination, caused by the strike in France, precluded the need for any relief from the heat, so our swimsuits remained tucked away in our luggage.

Belle Island guards the entrance to the St. Lawrence Seaway near the eastern-most reaches of the Canadian province of Newfoundland and Labrador. This was our first land sighting since departing France and served to heighten our anticipation of what we hoped would be a reunion with Mom and Dad. The General *Madalinski* hugged the shoreline of Quebec Province as we made our way down the river to Port Cartier.

Immediately after securing the ship in port, the covers of the massive holds were pulled back to accommodate the dumping of grain from a huge conveyor belt. The process was to continue non-stop for the next thirty-six hours, during which time Ewa and I were to disembark. We were called to the Captain's office where we met with the shipping agent. He knew we were passengers on the vessel and in possession of some crates which required land transport. He had arranged for a trucking company to remove the crates and deliver them to Des Moines. We signed some papers and were returning to our cabin when one of the crew members stopped Ewa to ask if her father-in-law was handicapped in any way. He told Ewa that an unidentified man with a pronounced limp was climbing the gangway. We were quite certain it was not my father but made our way to the deck to see for ourselves.

"Look, it *is* Dad!" Ewa exclaimed.

I have rarely been so happy to see someone. After hugs and greetings, Mom joined us for a brief tour of our living accommodations aboard the ship. It was agreed that Mom and Dad would return to the ship early the next morning, when we would pack the car with our eleven suitcases and head for Des Moines. The remainder of the day was filled with individual good-byes shared with the ship's officers and crew.

Our destination for the first night was the city of Quebec. The drive was long, but the time went fast as we had much to talk about. Fortunately, there was only one main highway to Quebec, which rendered moot the fact that all signage was written only in French. Of course, I knew Quebec was the most French of all Canadian provinces, but I was unaware as to just how French it was. Though there was always someone around who spoke English, French—or more accurately, Canadian French—was the language of choice. Even my untrained ear could discern a difference in the language as I had heard it in Rouen and that which I was hearing in Quebec.

Think of American English as contrasted with British English and you have the idea. The four of us would have loved to spend some time touring the city, but we had a long way to travel. We checked into a cheap hotel, enjoyed a filling meal and retired to bed.

We awoke bright and early the next day with a plan to make Buffalo, New York, our end point for the day. The plan was an optimistic one, given the five hundred fifty miles between the two cities and the international border to be negotiated along the way. We traveled down the Canadian side of the St. Lawrence River through Montreal, and remained in Canada until crossing into the United States at Wellesley Island in upstate New York.

This was to be Ewa's first US port of entry as Mrs. Timothy Pratt. Here she displayed her Polish passport, our marriage certificate, and some official papers provided by the US Embassy in Warsaw which indicated she was the spouse of a US citizen. At that time, this meant she would be granted a Green Card and authorized work status as a permanent resident alien. It appeared as if the processing of a brand new immigrant was not a daily occurrence at this port of entry. The administrative detail took only about an hour and was a painless, almost enjoyable experience. We wondered if the experience would have been the same had we entered through Texas or California, and concluded it might have been less pleasant.

We continued on through the beautiful Thousand Islands region of New York toward Syracuse, and then on to Buffalo. "Beautiful" seems the appropriate modifier for this part of New York, though perhaps it is a bit too modest. I have chosen the path of understatement because, all too frequently, one uses only superlatives or hyperbole when describing the beauty and grandeur of places one has visited. Who comments on the Grand Canyon with phrases like, "it was pretty," or "the sunset was neat?" No, the Grand Canyon was "the most incredible thing I have ever seen," or "the sunset was a merger of the most intense shades of purple, orange, and blue on the western horizon." Upstate New York was indeed very beautiful and we hope to return there someday.

Our sense of anticipation was growing. We were now in the United States and only two days from finally establishing our own home in Des Moines. This day's itinerary would take us from Buffalo, New York to Chicago, via Niagara Falls. Not wanting to risk any border delays which might jeopardize our Chicago arrival, we stayed on the US side of the falls. We took a few pictures and stayed long enough so we could tell people we had been there, but not enough time to truly appreciate the wonder of nature that is Niagara Falls. Nine hours later we were dining with Clif and Lucille in Chicago. This was a homecoming of sorts for Ewa, as this was where she had spent her first night in the US on her initial visit in 1976. The next evening would be spent in our own apartment.

Chapter 10: Home Sweet Home With Papal Blessings

My paternal grandfather, Rollo, passed away in his sleep during the summer of 1964. He was living with my grandmother, Vada, in a duplex on Easton Boulevard in Des Moines when he died. The duplex had been purchased a few years earlier by my Uncle Vern. Vern's first wife, Roberta, had passed away at the age of forty five, leaving him as a single parent to two teenage children. This property allowed for him and his kids (Fred and Margo) to live on one side while his parents (Rollo and Vada) occupied the other. As an over-the-road truck driver, Uncle Vern was sometimes away from home, and this arrangement permitted his parents to perform parental responsibilities in his absence.

Grandma Vada (Grandma Pratt, as we referenced her) continued to live there for several years after my grandfather's death. Over the next decade, Vern remarried (LaVanche), cousins Fred and Margo married and moved out, and my grandmother moved to an assisted living facility. Vern had moved into LaVanche's home. The duplex was now a rental property and one side of the property was vacant. I had agreed to rent the available space from Uncle Vern upon our return from Poland. This was our destination as we left Clif and Lucille in Chicago.

It was August 1st, 1979, when we arrived in Des Moines and set up housekeeping at 2601 Easton Boulevard. The day after we arrived in Des Moines I walked across the street to the K-mart to purchase a sufficiently-mushy card to mark our upcoming first anniversary. While at the store, I learned of the tragic death of one of my all-time favorite baseball players, Thurman Munson, who had perished in a plane crash in Ohio. Munson was a catcher for the New York Yankees. I was, and still am, a Yankee fan, and I, too, was a catcher. This bit of trivia has no significant relevance to this story. Nevertheless, I feel compelled to share it to somehow memorialize a very good baseball player.

We had a couple of weeks before football practice started and school resumed. This time was used to secure teaching credentials, a driver's license, and job applications for Ewa. It was also a time to introduce her to the basics of bill-paying, credit cards, and general consumer finance—US-style. Please understand, Ewa has never had a problem with budgets, living within her means, or being accountable for where her money goes. In fact, though I am the designated bill payer in our family, she is considerably more attentive to these matters than am I. It's just that she had never had a checking account to balance, or a credit card, or ever taken a commercial loan. These concepts were all new to her, as was evidenced a few short weeks after we arrived in Des Moines. We received an "overdraft" notice from our bank.

"This means we spent more money than we have in our account," I explained to Ewa.

"Wow, you can do that here,?!" came her reply.

"No, honey, we can't. That's why the bank is sending us this notice. Our check bounced. This means the bank didn't honor the check we wrote to the store."

"We didn't have that problem back in Poland. My parents had a series of envelopes: one for rent, one for groceries, and one for other expenses. Each payday, Dad would put the appropriate amounts in the rent and groceries envelopes, keep a little cash for himself, and the rest went into the remaining envelope. If the envelopes were empty, we did without, or he borrowed from a friend until payday. It was all pretty simple."

As I reflect on that conversation today, I have to wonder if the system implemented by Sylwester and Maria Domagała would have better served the global economy than what has been used over the past thirty years.

The new school year had just begun. Our first football game was scheduled for the next Friday. Ewa had already been working as a substitute teacher. Despite the minor mishap where she hit the lone parked car in the otherwise empty Saydel High School parking lot, Ewa's driving acumen was improving. We were adjusting to cohabitation and life as Mr. and Mrs. Pratt. Life was pretty good as we settled in to some semblance of a routine. Then Dad called to tell us the Pope was coming to Iowa. That's right, the same fellow who had followed me to Poland a few weeks earlier was now pursuing me on my home turf. Fearing pox, plague, or a lifetime diet of strawberries if we chose to do otherwise, I circled Thursday October 4th on the calendar and promised Ewa we would go to see him.

Joe Hays, a farmer from rural Truro, Iowa, had written a personal letter to invite Pope John Paul II to the Heartland of America. Mr. Hays was a parishioner at tiny St. Patrick's Church in Cumming, Iowa, a mere ten miles from the southwestern edge of Des Moines. The Pope had agreed to visit the tiny church and to follow with an open-air mass on the grounds of Living History Farms.

The Pope's acceptance of Mr. Hays's invitation infused the community with an energy I had not seen before, and have not witnessed since. Security had to be planned. Interstate highways would be closed. Portable toilets were needed for 350,000 people. The presidential helicopter would be on loan to transport the Pope while he was here. Would businesses allow for time off? Who would cover the costs for the event? Would the schools close? This was a religious event that required cooperation from much more than the local Catholic Diocese. Church and state came together to partner with the private sector in addressing the logistics of this event. The Pope was a foreign Head of State. City, county, state and federal governments were each assigned tasks and did their parts. The private sector donated money and people to aid in the administration of the event. The mass was planned by the local Diocese with the Pope's representatives from the Vatican. Even the Polish community of Des Moines had a role in the day's activities. It was agreed that one person, selected by the local Polish community, would greet the Pope as he arrived via helicopter at Living History Farms.

The Polish community in Des Moines in 1979 was pretty small. It consisted primarily of second generation Poles whose families had immigrated to the US at the turn of the century and subsequently made their way from Chicago's packing houses to Des Moines, and a few other families who had arrived here following World War II. It was an informal group which held potlucks at Christmas and Easter, and a summer picnic. When we learned of the Pope's planned visit to Iowa, the ruling "committee" called for a hasty gathering of all Poles in the greater metro area to determine who would be selected to greet the Holy Father in his native tongue. After a very spirited discussion, the field was narrowed to two young girls. Following a brief interview by the "committee" to determine command of the Polish language and social etiquette, Dorota Rokitnicki was chosen to represent the Polish community as Pope John Paul II arrived at Living History Farms. Dorota was about ten years old and she was the niece of our friends, Lola and Waldek Darowski (the ones with whom we share the same wedding day).

If you are like me, you may take for granted some of the more interesting venues in your home community. Only when you have out-of-town company do you seek out some of those attractions, and then come away thinking, "That was pretty cool. I should come here more often." Living History Farms is just such a place.

As its name implies, it is a "living" museum of farms from three different time periods; 1800, 1850, and 1900. Each farm is manned by employees who, for eight hours each day, dress, work, and live as people did during the time of the farm where they are working. It was first made available to the public in 1970, and its wide expanse of rolling prairie was a perfect setting for the Pope's open-air mass.

In the days leading up to the Pope's arrival we learned that Hickman Road, the primary access route to Living History Farms, would be closed at 10:00 PM on the night before the mass. We met with Lola and Waldek to plan our strategy to be as near as possible to the Pontiff during mass. We decided to take some food and water, warm clothes, blankets, and a couple of plastic trash bags, which would double as raincoats in the event of inclement weather. We agreed it was best to arrive at Living History Farms before Hickman Road was closed down.

We parked our cars a couple of miles away and had my father drop us off at the entrance to Living History Farms right at 10:00 PM Wednesday evening. The Holy Father was scheduled to arrive there in the early afternoon the following day.

Iowa winters can be brutal, but having already experienced twenty-four of them, I was confident we could easily meet the challenges of a lone early fall evening while exposed to the elements. I failed to consider, however, that in the prior twenty-four years I had never remained outside for nineteen consecutive hours without seeking temporary refuge in a car, home, or warming hut. I can now bear witness that thirty degrees, accompanied by even a ten mile-per-hour wind, is cold. And it gets colder with each passing hour. And being cold somehow activates the bladder. I'll share more on that subject a little later.

Organizers had established barriers of single ropes, accompanied by intermittent volunteers whose job it was to tell the crowd to remain behind one line of rope until instructed to advance to the next line of rope. At 10:00 PM, the crowd consisted of less than fifty people. By 2:00 AM, when we were allowed to advance about two hundred yards to the next rope barrier, I think there were several hundred. I couldn't be certain how many people there were because it was pitch dark. Temporary floodlights had been set up near the entrance to the museum and we could make out a few flashlights.

A group of about ten college kids, both male and female, settled about twenty-five yards from us. They had come prepared with blankets, a guitar, and liquid refreshment. They began singing some of the classics of Peter, Paul, and Mary, and other appropriately mellow offerings. On the way back from one of my numerous trips to the portable toilet, I stopped long enough to learn they had driven all day from South Bend, Indiana. As students at the University of Notre Dame they figured they could come and see the Pope in Des Moines on Thursday, and still return in time for Saturday's football game against Georgia Tech. I thought to myself, "Oh, to be back in school, again," and wondered if their parents knew about this little road trip.

Less than ten minutes after returning to join Ewa, Lola, Waldek, and Lucinda Borel (a former neighbor who also went with us that evening), a fragrance of unambiguous origin began to permeate our circle. Lucinda and I began to laugh when, after sniffing the air like an English bloodhound in search of the elusive convict, my wife inquired of Lola and Waldek, "What is that smell?" Neither of them could identify it. You guessed it. Our road-tripping Fighting Irish coeds and friends were smoking dope right there on the grounds of Living History Farms while waiting for Pope John Paul II. I wondered if they ever felt the need to confess this transgression, or did they think a sixteen hour round trip to see the Holy Father was sufficient penance for smoking a couple of doobies?

At 6:00 AM we were allowed to advance to the next rope. Day was breaking and we could see the crowd numbered in the thousands. It was cold and overcast, with very brief occasions of sunlight. At 10:00 AM we were permitted to proceed to the final barrier, which still was at least fifty yards from the temporary altar where mass would be recited. We were as close to His Holiness as one could be, excepting those who were participants in the formal mass.

No longer were there volunteers posted at intervals on the other side of the ropes. Those stations were now manned by secret service agents and local police. Directly across from us was a female secret service agent. She looked the part: well dressed, long beige trench coat, sunglasses, and I am confident she was "packing heat," though I was unable to visually confirm this. While she never entered into a real conversation with us, she occasionally responded to our questions.

"Has the Pope landed at the airport, yet?"
"Yes."
"Are you really Secret Service?"
"Yes."
"How about those Redskins?"

No response, but I did get a little smile. By now the crowd had grown to a quarter million, or more, and we were in the front row. This wasn't nearly as glamorous as one might think because all of those people were between me and the portable toilets—and I was in desperate need of a urinal. Lola had visited the bathroom soon after we had advanced to the final station and she was gone for ninety minutes. As I looked out over the gathering masses I concluded two things: I probably would not make it all the way to the toilet before relieving myself, and, if I did manage to make it to bathroom, there was no way I would return to this position before the Pope arrived. I shared my dilemma with Ewa. Her response was simple, direct, and altogether insufficient.

"Don't drink any more liquids."
"Thank you, Dear. I also won't cross the street when cars are coming." Clearly, I was on my own in resolving this matter.

Mom always taught me that "necessity is the mother of invention." Much like that scene in the movie, *Apollo XIII*, where the NASA engineers were brought into a room, shown everything that was on board the space capsule, and asked to design a makeshift filter to remove the carbon dioxide from the air supply to the astronauts while they circled the earth, I began to assess my resources and my options. We had a one gallon water thermos with spigot which was about one third full, a couple of Oreo cookies in a ziplock container, two empty plastic Glad sandwich bags, one sleeve of Ritz crackers still in the cardboard box, a folding chair, some blankets and two Hefty trash can liners. This was a "MacGyver" moment (though I don't think he even existed then) if there ever was one.

While conversing with "Secret Service Sally" I asked Ewa for one of the Hefty trash can liners. The wind had picked up a little and there had been a few sprinkles of rain. I pulled the trash bag over my head and poked holes for both arms and my head. I was now wearing the trash bag as a makeshift raincoat. It all seemed plausible.

I wore this "slicker" for a period just long enough to sell the idea to all around me. After a few minutes I removed the slicker, opting to use the trash bag as a windbreaker by stepping into it, and cinching the drawstring around my waist. The "windbreaker" now had a hole in the bottom where my head had been in the "slicker." I was about to experience that rare combination of exhilaration and relief which results in near euphoria. Right there in the front row of a crowd larger than the entire population of Des Moines, while making small talk with a female secret service agent and awaiting the arrival of the most revered person in all of Christendom, I reached inside my windbreaker, unzipped my fly, and nearly flooded our little section of Living History Farms.

Thirty minutes later I asked Ewa for a drink of water from the thermos. She refused, citing our earlier conversation. I conceded she was right and decided to wait until the mass was over to tell her how I had solved my problem.

Word spread throughout the crowd that the Pope had just boarded the helicopter at St. Patrick's in Cumming, Iowa and would soon be with us. The landing area was about two hundred yards to our left and our view was blocked by the people. We couldn't see much but we managed to catch a glimpse of little Dorota in her native Polish costume. The next morning's newspaper had some great photos of her presenting flowers to Karol Wojtyła, the former Archbishop of Kraków, aka Pope John Paul II.

Stewardship of the land was a central theme of the mass. To be honest I don't recall a lot of the service, but I do remember the little girl standing on the backs of my ankles as we were kneeling.

Her father had put her on his shoulders, but when others behind them complained, he apparently thought my Achilles tendons offered just enough elevation for her to see.

As was his custom *before* the assassination attempt on his life, John Paul II made his way toward the crowd who had gathered to see him. He was accompanied by several Secret Service personnel as he walked along the edge of the rope barriers. Ewa and Lola began calling out "*Święty Ojciec*" (Holy Father) in an effort to attract his attention. He must have heard them because he altered his direction and was coming straight toward us. Like everyone else, I held out my hand hoping to touch him. He was less than ten feet from us when one of the Secret Service agents gently turned him with the words, "This way Holy Father."

All of us were excited and disappointed at the same time. Privately, I wondered if being within ten feet of the Pope would help us win the next night's football game against Grinnell. It didn't. I think we lost 32-6. Maybe the Grinnell coach was in the crowd that day and actually touched him.

With the day's festivities coming to a close we made the long trek up Hickman Road to our car... and to the rest of our life together.

The journey back to the car afforded me the opportunity to reflect on how our lives had changed in the previous four and a half years. I had been a school bus driver who had never been on a plane. Now, I was leaving an open air mass, led by the Pope, with my Polish wife. I had traveled to Europe three times. Ewa had been to the US three times. We had endured numerous lengthy separations. We had received a personal response to a letter I had written to the President of the United States. Was the random nature of events truly random? A speeding ticket and an interest in barbershop music led to a trip on a freighter and a visit to where Joan of Arc is burned at the stake? I guess I was pondering what we now reference as the "butterfly effect." Call it destiny, divine guidance, pre-ordination, fate, or just plain old luck. All I knew with certainty was that I had been very blessed.

Epilogue

Much has transpired in the thirty plus years since that fall day in 1979. The map of Europe has been altered. Walls have been torn down, both literally and figuratively, with the forming of the European Union. New walls have been erected to keep people out of the United States. We have a different Pope. The Cold War has been displaced by different global conflicts, and it is sometimes hard to identify certain countries based solely on the ideologies of their governments. Yet, for all of the changes, some things have remained constant. I still get gooseflesh when a championship barbershop quartet rings a perfect four-part chord. My father still likes to sing. I occasionally drive too fast. I can still coach football. The friends I referenced in this book are still my friends. I enjoy each return trip to Poland. Ewa has added Spanish to her linguistic repertoire, and she still does not suffer fools well. My wife seeks to improve at something every day, and she inspires me to be more than I might otherwise be. Above all else, I continue to be glad that I married her, and I look forward to the next thirty years.

Tim & Ewa Pratt

Visit Our Website

Join Our Mailing List

A fantastic new way to keep up-to-date with the Pratts!
Our Newsletter is a regular email with all the latest news and views
from the author, plus information on his forthcoming titles and the
chance to win exclusive prizes.

Just go to www.mylifewithewa.com and type your email address
in the 'Join our newsletter' panel.
Then, fill in your details and you will be added to Tim's list.

Library Tales Publishing

If you enjoyed this book, there are several ways you can read more by the same author and make sure you get the inside track on all Library Tales Publishing books.

Visit www.librarytalespublishing.com and find out first about forthcoming titles, read exclusive material and author interviews, and enter exciting competitions.

You can also browse through thousands of Library Tales Publishing books and buy online.

It's never been easier to read more with Library Tales Publishing.

Library Tales Publishing
www.librarytalespublishing.com